Evolution of Consciousness

Evolution of Consciousness

The Philosophy of Pierre Teilhard
de Chardin and the Evolutionary
Transformation Unfolding Within Us

Threshold to Meaning Series
Book One

VINCENT FRANK BEDOGNE

WIPF & STOCK · Eugene, Oregon

EVOLUTION OF CONSCIOUSNESS
The Philosophy of Pierre Teilhard de Chardin and the Evolutionary
Transformation Unfolding Within Us

Threshold to Meaning, Book 1

Wipf & Stock
A Division of Wipf and Stock Publishers
199 W. 8th Ave., Suite 3
Eugene, OR 97401

www.wipfandstock.com

ISBN 13: 978-1-55635-924-8

Manufactured in the U.S.A.

To My Father

A truth once seen, even by a single mind, always ends up by imposing itself on the totality of human consciousness.

Pierre Teilhard de Chardin,
The Phenomenon of Man

Contents

Series Introduction

OVER TIME, CERTAIN IDEAS and individuals stand out as pivotal to human progress. One thinks of Niels Bohr, who in the early twentieth century proposed his model of atomic structure and thus established the basis for quantum mechanics, and Albert Einstein, who in that same timeframe proposed his special and general theories of relativity. Earlier names include the founders of modern electrical and magnetic theory Michael Faraday and James Clark Maxwell and, of course, Newton, Galileo, and Copernicus. The advances made by these individuals, and others across the disciplines, have one thing in common. Each builds on the knowledge that preceded it. The physics of quantum mechanics and relativity theory rests on the electrical models of Faraday and Maxwell and on the classical mechanics of Newton. Newton was influenced by the empirical science of Galileo, who was influenced by the heliocentric model of the solar system proposed by Copernicus, who was influenced by Ptolemy's geocentric system of planetary motion. In the first half of the twentieth century, the paleontologist and Jesuit priest Pierre Teilhard de Chardin drew on the sciences and philosophies in the most comprehensive way imaginable. Teilhard proposed a fundamentally different view of humanity and the universe—a vision that many if not most who are familiar with it, including such thinkers as Rene Hague and Sir Julian Huxley, see as pivotal to human progress.

Above all, Teilhard sought to account for the totality of the human experience in a single, coherent explanation of the universe. To be true to reality, such an explanation would have to embrace the behavior and evolution of life and of the cosmos as observed and understood by science and the less tangible qualities of the human experience that many if not most of us take for granted: specifically our belief in and experience of a god, soul, and afterlife. In a no less comprehensive way, Teilhard felt, can we ever fundamentally understand the universe and the role humankind and we as individuals occupy in the universe.

Driven by this conviction, Teilhard accepted the fossil evidence of organic evolution but felt that organic change over time did not take place through the random process of natural selection proposed by Charles Darwin. Inspired by Henri Bergson's *Creative Evolution*, Teilhard theorized that another mechanism accounted for evolution—the *creative process*, the same creative mechanism that we experience within ourselves. In Teilhard's view, a common process underlies the birth of a star, the evolution of a species, the writing of a play or novel, and the invention and development of a scientific theory. This realization led Teilhard to an even more startling conclusion. If the universe evolved through the creative process, its fundamental nature could not be as the evolution of matter that science takes to be absolute and is devoted to understanding. Teilhard saw the universe as an *evolution of consciousness* that in the beginning and at every level of its organization manifested in an evolution of matter.

In the late 1950s and early 1960s, Teilhard's evolution of consciousness view drew a great deal of popular and academic interest. His ideas tied together our fragmented understanding of the universe in an overall picture of evolution. But, as the years past, Teilhard's vision fell into obscurity. Organized religion dismissed Teilhard's ideas because they challenged scriptural notions of creation. Science dismissed Teilhard's ideas because they challenged Darwinism and suggested that the universe's fundamental nature could not be quantified and boiled down to an equation. The Jesuit's vision may have been intriguing and may have rang-true on an intuitive level, but it fell short in one way. Teilhard could not explain how the creative process functioned, how his "evolution of consciousness" took place.

The book in hand—*Threshold to meaning: Book 1, Evolution of consciousness*—is the first in a series of three titles that advance the ideas of Pierre Teilhard de Chardin to their next logical level. In the first work, I begin with Teilhard's vision of the universe and go on to propose a simple mechanism, the *Creative Process*, that in a specific and highly pragmatic way explains how our universe, taken to be an evolution of consciousness, manifests in the evolution of matter we see around us and that clearly took place in the past. So simple and defined is this process that the reader—from scientist to spiritualist—will be on the comfortable ground of logic and reasoned development. I then offer an account of the universe's origin, evolution, and future as it appears in light of the creative process—an inspiring and optimistic look at our world, ourselves, and where we are headed. With all due reverence, I think of the first book in the series as the work Teilhard would have written had he lived another fifty years and incorporated the latter twentieth century's advances into his thinking.

This, however, is only the beginning. A philosophical undertaking of Teilhardian scope lends insight into many areas. In *Threshold to Meaning: Book 2, Economics of Fulfillment*, I look at one of the key topics brought into focus by the account of the universe presented in the first book, one that touches our lives in a direct way—economics. At present, every nation embraces a blend of two major economic philosophies: socialism and capitalism. In light of our "Threshold to Meaning" understanding of the universe, we see economics in all its past and contemporary forms—those that lean toward socialism and those that lean toward capitalism—as obsolete. A new economic philosophy reveals itself, an economics for tomorrow—an economics of fulfillment.

As profound as humanity's move beyond socialism and capitalism may be, economic reformation is nothing more than the advance that will allow us to progress in an even more remarkable direction. In *Threshold to Meaning: Book 3, Blueprint for Reconstruction,* we discuss what economics of fulfillment will make it possible for humanity to achieve—perfection of life on Earth. We describe our rebuilding of what I call the Earth's urban and ecological infrastructure: the city of tomorrow, the countryside of tomorrow, how we will get around and communicate. We adopt a new environmentalism, explore future sources of energy, reveal the solution to humanity's present energy crisis, and look at how we will build for a changing climate and biosphere.

By their nature, certain ideas presented in this series of books—in particular those developed in the first volume, *Evolution of Consciousness,* which deal with time, space, and the creative process—are abstract. The books are intended to be serious philosophical works. But they are not written strictly for the scientist or philosopher. I have gone to great lengths to make the most difficult concepts understandable. The books are accessible to anyone interested in the essential human questions of who we are and how and for purpose we came to be, and who is willing to put the thought into their understanding that such questions imply. How true to reality would any fundamental understanding of the universe be if accessible only to the few? Humanity and thus the universe cannot attain its highest level of achievement until every human being attains his or her highest level of achievement. The universe's threshold to meaning unfolds within each of us.

Illustrations

Preface

IN THE HUMAN PURSUIT of meaning—in our universal endeavor to comprehend existence and to forge for ourselves a place within—we often seek guidance in the philosophies. Untold are the number of individuals who have aspired to understanding through reflection on the world's religious teachings. Untold are the number who have aspired to knowledge through study of the theoretical edifices fostered by science. Among the many philosophical orders that enrich the human experience, there is one that, as I believe those who are most familiar with it would agree, stands poised to impact our future in a fundamental way. Like all belief systems, this philosophy builds on the wisdom that preceded it. Like the greatest, it employs that wisdom to thrust our view of life and universe in a new direction. It is a turning point in thought that has stirred passions of loyalty and controversy for more than fifty years. It is a pivotal shift in perspective that today compels us to look at our universe and ourselves in a different way and by doing so to face a startling possibility.

To understand this possibility and the view that led to its development, we must return to the spring of 1955—and to the death of an extraordinary man. His name was *Pierre Teilhard de Chardin*. He was a scientist and philosopher. His death made possible the publication of one of the twentieth century's most thought provoking books.

By profession, Teilhard was a paleontologist. He spent his life venturing across the deserts of Ethiopia, the rain forests of Java, throughout Burma, China, Africa, and Mongolia. His passion to comprehend the nature and meaning of existence, though, led him beyond the field of geology to the study of human evolution. He examined the Australopithecus finds of Raymond Dart and Robert Broom in Africa. He took part in many of the twentieth century's greatest archaeological expeditions. He was there when Davidson Black's team in China unearthed Peking Man. Yet, Teilhard was not only a distinguished scientist.

He was also a Jesuit Priest well known for his intellectual contributions to Catholicism. Perhaps driven by some inner conflict between world views, perhaps driven by a mission to understand more gripping than his love of faith or his admiration for science, both of which he embraced with all his being, Teilhard founded and sought to inspire the development of a markedly different view of humanity and the universe.

His vision shocked science and theology. In a rare moment of agreement, the two forces of Western intellect joined hands to denounce the Jesuit and his beliefs. As a result of this condemnation, the church banned Teilhard from publishing his philosophical works. Embattled throughout much of his career, distraught during his later years but of a character unwilling to break the vow of obedience that as a young man he had made to the church, Teilhard entrusted his writings to a friend for publication after death.

On Easter Sunday, 1955, Teilhard passed away. Suppressed for almost two decades, the volume widely held to be his most revealing work, *The Phenomenon of Man*, saw print within months.

What threatened the reigning powers of thought to such a degree as to compel them to silence the lone priest was the most dramatic departure from their respective views since Charles Darwin proposed his theory of organic evolution through the process of natural selection almost a century earlier. Central to *Teilhardian* philosophy, the foundation of which he most comprehensively presents in *The Phenomenon of Man*, are four concepts.

The first and most fundamental is the conviction that we as human beings are capable of understanding the nature and meaning of the universe. Across the spectrum of thought, many consider the least tangible aspects of the human experience beyond explanation. Theologians contend that we, as mere human beings, are not equipped to comprehend God. Such an entity is too far removed from everyday life for us to internalize and deal with. Similarly, many in science hypothesize that the universe began as an infinitely hot and dense point that exploded to create the cosmos, the big bang model of cosmic formation. When asked what created the infinitely hot and dense point, science offers no explanation other than to say that such falls outside the domain of science. Teilhard felt that—as beings who think and learn as we do—we are not only capable of understanding the universe's nature and meaning, we are obligated to understand it. Nothing is beyond the human ability to grasp. To comprehend the universe's nature and meaning is our highest role, that which by our existence we are driven to achieve.

The second of Teilhard's foundational concepts is the notion of an *evolving universe*. Like many scientists and philosophers, Teilhard defined evolution in a simple way: as the change over time of an earlier, more primitive state of existence, organic or otherwise, into a later, more advanced state. But here his vision departs. Like today, most scientists and philosophers of Teilhard's time saw the universe as shaped by distinct types of evolution: namely cosmic, biological, and social-cultural evolution. Because cosmic evolution created the conditions necessary for biological evolution to take place, which made social-cultural evolution possible, Teilhard felt that this could not be the case. He reasoned that what at first appear to be separate, unrelated evolutions must be stages in a single, greater evolution. Teilhard saw one line of evolutionary advance—a universe in transformation from a simple, primitive state of existence into a complex, advanced state. "The universe in its entirety," as Sir Julian Huxley described Teilhard's view,[1] "must be regarded as one gigantic process, a process of becoming, of attaining new levels of existence and organization . . ."

The third basic concept of Teilhardian philosophy is the idea of *evolutionary context*. If we accept Teilhard's notion of an evolving universe, it follows that to fully understand the universe's evolution we must examine it from its beginning. Consequently, to grasp the purpose of an event that furthered the universe's evolution—whether that event be the arrangement of atoms to create the first molecule, the organization of communities to create the first city, or today's uncertain global economic conditions—we must examine it with reference to its origin in time, or evolutionary position. Though for certain purposes it may be useful to see an event as isolated in time, an event viewed out of evolutionary context—like a scene in a movie played out of sequence—appears less than whole. To truly understand our existence we must examine ourselves in the light of all that came before, in the context of the universe's evolution.

The fourth basic concept of Teilhardian philosophy is the idea of *intrinsic consciousness*. Traditionally, scientists have regarded matter as

1. Teilhard de Chardin, *The Phenomenon of Man*, 13.

the basic substance of the universe. They have seen consciousness as the result of the organization of matter, present only in life. Teilhard reasoned that in an evolving universe consciousness could not thus appear. He felt that for awareness to be present today, it, like the more primitive arrangements of matter that underlie organic structure, must have been present in some form before the advent of life. He felt that the human awareness we experience evolved from increasingly primitive levels of consciousness, traceable back in time through the organic and into the inorganic. Farfetched? Perhaps. But does not the physicist interpret atomic structure as sustained by an exchange of "information" between particles, and can we not infer from this view that such an exchange represents a rudimentary awareness of one subatomic particle's relationship to another? Teilhard believed that to understand our universe, we must examine it at all levels not only from the standpoint of matter but also from the standpoint of consciousness.

Taken together, the basic concepts of Teilhardian philosophy comprise a way of looking at ourselves and our universe popularly termed the *evolution of consciousness* view. This view has been the topic of countless books, papers, and discussions and has the most staggering of implications; it would fundamentally change the way we see our universe and ourselves. But despite the view's potential, most scholars dismiss it for one reason. In the fifty or more years of the view's existence, no one has explained how a universe whose nature is as an evolution of consciousness could manifest in a universe observed to be as an evolution of matter.

This brings us to the present book. My goal in the following pages is twofold. First, I propose a theoretical mechanism that I believe resolves the above issue. I outline a simple and highly plausible process that I believe explains how our universe, taken to be as an evolution of consciousness, manifests as the evolution of matter we see around us and that clearly took place in the past. As for the second part of the book's objective, I offer an account of the universe's origin, development, and future as—based on many years of research and reflection—I believe it would appear in light of our fundamental unifying process.

In Part One, *Emergence*, and in Chapter One, *Emptiness*, which precedes and establishes the first part of the book, we travel back in time some fifteen billion years.[2] There we examine the state of "void," that, so

2. Cosmologists estimate that the universe is between seven and twenty billion years old. I represent this range by the traditionally publicized figure of fifteen billion years. At

we deduce, we must confront as the universe's initial condition, and outline the mechanism by which such a state could have given rise to time and space.

In Part Two, *Structure*, we highlight the universe's evolution from emergence to a point about four billion years ago. We further develop the theoretical process that unites matter and consciousness, look at the formation of atomic, molecular, and cosmic structure, and reconcile our evolution of consciousness account to science's big bang model and other physical theory.

In Part Three, *Life*, we examine the universe's evolution as advanced through biological development. We explore the trend of increasing organic complexity and consciousness to see life's progress as driven not by Darwinian natural selection but by the same elemental creative process that drove all prior evolution.

In Part Four, *Understanding*, we examine the universe's evolution as advanced through the growth of human knowledge. We begin at the time of humanity's first reflective thought—that mysterious moment when the first human being became aware of its own consciousness—and progress until we reach the modern world—life as we know it seen in evolutionary context.[3]

In Part Five, *Fulfillment*, we examine the universe's future and the human role in its attainment. We look at the emergence of a new economic philosophy and at the rebuilding of the Earth's urban and ecological infrastructure—and speculate on the ultimate state to which our analysis suggests evolution must carry us.

As we traverse from past to future, one observation cannot escape our attention. The evolution of consciousness view draws our study of the universe's evolution in on ourselves. We come to see that humanity occupies a special place in the scheme of things. We no longer envision ourselves as the static center of the universe as often professed to by religion, nor as the accident of nature as often professed to by science, but in a far more compelling way: in Teilhard's words, "as the axis and leading shoot of evolution, which is something much finer."[4]

---

the time of this writing, however, the scientific community may be settling in on a figure closer to fourteen billion years.

3. Humanity's crossing of the threshold to reflection is a key concept that will be dealt with at length.

4. Teilhard de Chardin, *The Phenomenon of Man*, 36.

As it must, this observation forces us to confront a startling possibility. Along with the importance it assigns humanity, the major outcome of the book's analysis is the significance it places on our present moment in evolution. Each chapter draws us to the conclusion that the universe is, as Teilhard foresaw, at an evolutionary turning point. Not at some indeterminate time in the future but now, as I write these words, the universe is undergoing a fundamental transformation. And this transformation is taking place within us.

Consciousness as we know it is changing. Human awareness is reshaping to, in a way unlike what we are familiar, embrace and align with the great movement that is the universe. I call this turning point in evolution the *threshold to meaning*. As meaning unfolds within us, we accept our position as at the forefront of the universe's advance. With the wind of all prior time at our backs, we march forward. Soul-by-soul, we ascend. Empowered by a new and profoundly human vision, we cross the threshold into a future nothing less than wondrous.

Acknowledgments

L IKE ANY WORK OF this type, research and writing take place over many years and involve many people along the way. I wish to express my gratitude to all with whom I have interacted. The following are those individuals who helped with the manuscript's preparation or had the greatest influence on my thoughts: Bill Lyon, James Bowen, Dawn Kohler, Marcy Everest, Carrie Wolcott, and Gene Landsmann. I would also like to thank my family, my mother, and my father, Doctor Frank Bedogne, who gave me a copy of Teilhard's *The Phenomenon of Man* when I was in the seventh grade. Such may not say much for my adolescence, but it had a big impact on my life.

1

Emptiness

PERHAPS THE LEAST DISPUTED "fact" about the universe is that complex things are composed of simple things. Protons, neutrons, and electrons bind to make atoms, which fuse to make molecules, which clump to make stars and planets. Stars and planets arrange to form solar systems, which organize to form galaxies, which aggregate to form galactic clusters, which come together to form yet higher levels of cosmic organization. Organic molecules unite to create simple metabolic systems, which arrange to make cells, which unite to make organs and organisms. People bond to form families. Families group to make communities. Communities unite to create cities, and cities align to create states and nations. Thus, in an evolving universe—as most scientists and philosophers consider ours to be, where everything that now exists developed from something related but more primitive that once existed[1]—to look into the past is to reduce the universe to a simpler state.

As we look back in time, we see that social structure becomes less complex. The highly nestled and interwoven patterns of social organization and interaction seen in modern human societies meld into the less complex patterns of social bonding seen in early human societies, which meld into the yet more elemental patterns visible in non-human societies. Social structure grows less and less intricate, to beyond the emergence of the cell colony fade into the organic wash of a primal sea.

As we look back in time, we see that organic structure becomes simpler. The first single-celled entities emerged before the first multi-celled entities, which emerged before the first trees, fish, insects, reptiles, and mammals. Simple metabolic systems emerged before the earliest cells, which evolved to become organelles in later more complex cells. Beyond

---

1. See the Preface for an introduction to the concept of an "Evolving Universe."

the level of the organic molecule, life's structure as we typically define it vanishes, lost in a web of molecular interactions.

As we look back in time, we see that cosmic structure becomes less intricate. The first stellar bodies formed before the first galaxies. The first galaxies formed before the first galactic clusters, the first galactic clusters formed before the first clusters of galactic clusters, which formed before all higher levels of cosmic order. The first molecules came before the first stellar bodies. The first atoms came before the first molecules, and the first subatomic particles came before the first atoms.

The further back in time we look, the less complex a universe we see. Projection of this trend therefore allows us to deduce the existence of an initial simplest state, the least complex state we can possibly imagine, the universe's primordial seed, the point with which it all began—the state of existence we will call *emptiness*.

The notion of "emptiness" thrusts our analysis into the realm of the unexplored, for such a form of existence lies outside the domain of forms and states routinely addressed by science. To see why this is the case and to lay the foundation needed to explore the state of emptiness, we must establish certain ideas.

Foremost among these is a concept that scientists and philosophers from Saint Augustine to Albert Einstein have grappled with and that the twentieth century French thinker *Pierre Teilhard de Chardin*[2] developed to perhaps its most functional degree. This concept is the notion of the universe's *dual nature*.

What Teilhard and others realized as they contemplated the workings of existence is that it is often useful to think of the universe as existing on two levels: the *external* and the *internal*.[3]

For our purposes, the external is the physical or objective side of existence. It is social structure and patterns of social interaction. It is anatomy, organic structure, and biological function. It is the organization of the cosmos, the composition of the molecule, and the configuration of the atom. The external is time and space, matter in all its myriad of forms, and energy revealed through its interaction with matter. The external is that which we can map, plot, count, and statistically analyze.

2. See the Preface for a portrait of Pierre Teilhard de Chardin and for an introduction to Teilhardian philosophy.

3. Teilhard generally referred to the internal and the external as the "within" and the "without."

The internal is the nonphysical or subjective side of existence. It is love, intuition, and creativity. It is the awareness of self and surroundings that pervades life and that underlies social structure. It is the feelings that many have of the existence of a god or of some form of Supreme Being and of a soul and afterlife. The internal is that which we may experience and therefore know or believe to exist but cannot account for quantitatively or by other tangible means.

We often delegate the task of understanding the universe's internal aspects to theology. Science, on the other hand, directs its approach to explaining those aspects that we can weigh, measure, or in some way deal with externally.

To see why science chooses to direct its application in this way and to appreciate the consequence that such a choice may ultimately force science to confront, we must learn a little about the origin, development, and present state of science.

Throughout most of humankind's past, our ancestors made no real distinction between external and internal. The early Greeks, for example, thought of all matter as alive. They saw no difference between animate and inanimate, spirit and substance. About 2,300 years ago, this view began to change. At least in Western society, thoughts of body and Earth began to separate from thoughts of soul and creator. Spurred by the rise of this dichotomy, science came into existence as the tool we used to explain and control the external side of our world.

"Sweet and bitter, cold and warm, as well as all the colors," the Greek philosopher Democritus wrote in science's earliest days, "all these things exist but in opinion and not in reality; what really exists are unchangeable particles: atoms and their motions in empty space." Not long after, Aristotle, also a Greek philosopher, sought to explain the universe through self-evident principles. To Aristotle, it was self-evident, for example, that everything had its proper place. Objects fell to the ground because that was where they belonged, and smoke rose into the sky because that was where it belonged.

Science, in its "classical" sense, began in the seventeenth century when the Italian astronomer Galileo combined hypothesis, observation, and mathematics to originate the method of controlled experiment that to this day forms the basis of scientific investigation. Out of Galileo's advances and those of Isaac Newton a generation later there evolved a mechanical view of the universe—a cosmos of law and equation, of three-dimensional space and absolute time, of matter interacting through waves, forces, tensions, pressures, and oscillations.

Until the late 1800s, there seemed no physical process beyond the explanation of Newtonian mechanics, but science had only begun to grapple with matter at extremes of size and velocity. By the early twentieth century, small but key deviations between observed physical behavior and behavior as predicted by Newtonian law had become apparent. In response, there emerged the two great theoretical systems of modern physics: Einstein's special and general relativity, dealing with time, space, gravity, acceleration, and objects as they approached the speed of light, and quantum mechanics, dealing with waves and basic units of matter and energy. From these theories, a different view of the universe evolved—a cosmos of statistical probability, of flexible time and space, and of matter and energy interchangeability.

From the "atomistic" murmurs of Democritus to the development of modern physical theory, science's domain of investigation grew to embrace the external universe in an ever more comprehensive way. Today, we can describe science as the practice whereby we formulate a model, or abstract construct, of some aspect of the physical world, use that model to predict the aspect's behavior, and then wherever possible test our prediction against what we observe. The more closely our prediction agrees with what we see and measure the better we say is our understanding of the aspect in question. Given the power to control matter that science has yielded, we must conclude that this approach has been highly successful. But are we denying science its fullest expression?

Despite the strength of science as now practiced and the utility of the external-internal division, our choice to explore the world based on two isolated points of view has an outcome that by almost any line of reasoning is unavoidable. The question remains, can we expect either perspective alone to fully account for the universe? In this regard, Teilhard wrote:

> I am convinced that the two points of view [external and internal] . . . soon will unite . . . Otherwise, so it seems to me, it is impossible to cover the totality of the cosmic phenomenon by one coherent explanation such as science must try to construct.[4]

With this thought in mind, we return to our notion of emptiness. If Teilhard was correct in his assessment of external and internal and their

---

4. Teilhard de Chardin, *The Phenomenon of Man*, 53.

ultimate union, to probe the state of emptiness we must embrace the spirit and ideals of science—and the logic and supportability such embody—but push back the boundaries of scientific applicability. We must open ourselves to exploring the universe on an external and on an internal level. When we do so, a remarkable door opens. Viewed externally, emptiness appears empty—null, indefinable, the absolute void. Viewed internally, emptiness appears anything but empty.

Because emptiness exists on an internal level, we must explore it on that level. Emptiness has no expression in time and space, otherwise it would not be "empty" and therefore the simplest state imaginable, so we must look beyond the realm directly or, through technological enhancement, indirectly accessible to our external senses. This requires our use of a technique as old as human thought but, in a world dominated by science and its present focus on the tangible, rarely employed. To explore emptiness, we must look within ourselves.

As implausible as this idea may at first sound, it is grounded in an established line of reasoning. To see how we, in the present, can conceivably look within ourselves to learn about the origin of the universe, some fifteen billion[5] years in the past, we must take a closer look at the idea of evolution.

As we briefly discussed in the preface, most scientists and philosophers define evolution in a simple way: as the change over time of an earlier, more primitive state of existence, biological or otherwise, into a later, more advanced state. On this matter, Teilhard wrote:

> Nothing could ever burst forth as final across the different thresholds successively traversed by evolution (however critical they be) which has not already existed in an obscure and primordial way.[6]

Based on our definition of evolution, the past—by virtue of its role as progenitor of everything that came after—must be linked to the present. The universe as it was gave rise to and for this reason must be related to the universe as it is. It therefore follows that, in our quest to understand the universe, we can apply this relationship in two ways.

First, by examining the universe at a past evolutionary point, we can learn about the universe at its present evolutionary point. The geographer studies the age of European expansion to understand the modern

5. See the Preface, note 2.
6. Teilhard de Chardin, *The Phenomenon of Man*, 71.

dominance of Western culture. The horticulturist studies the emergence of agriculture to understand the genetic diversity of today's crops. The physicist studies the first milliseconds of existence to understand the later stages of cosmic evolution. The universe of yesterday is an open window into the universe of today.

And, second, by examining the universe at its present point in evolution, we can learn about it at a past point in its evolution. The anthropologist studies the modern hunting and gathering culture to understand the ancient hunting and gathering culture. The paleontologist studies the living species to understand the extinct species. The physicist uses relativity theory, developed to describe modern cosmic structure, to understand early cosmic structure. The universe of today is an open window into the universe of yesterday.

If our line of reasoning holds true, just as we can probe the universe's external make-up at earlier times through its present physical composition, we can probe the universe's internal make-up at earlier times through its present nonphysical composition. The universe's original state of emptiness would of course no longer exist, but some modern remnant or derivative of that state would seemingly be present. We would access it on the universe's internal level, and the most highly evolved expression of that level at hand is our own consciousness. Let us think about emptiness for a moment. Do we recognize this state?

The notion of emptiness initially brings to mind two conceptions, both limited. Those in, or exposed to, Western culture, where, as we mentioned, people tend to define the world externally, often think of emptiness as unoccupied space—the cosmic void. Those in, or exposed to, Eastern, Native American, or other culture with a more inward oriented tradition tend to think of emptiness as a mental state characterized by the absence of thought, often brought about by drugs, ritual, or meditation—the abandonment of self. Could both these notions be skirting a deeper meaning? What is the essential nature of emptiness?

We can grasp the underlying nature of emptiness through simple analysis and exploration of inner feeling. What, then, does emptiness feel like? When we experience emptiness, we experience a sensation of lack or absence. Emptiness is a hollow feeling in the chest or stomach. We may describe it as boredom or loneliness. It is a sense of void, an awareness that something in our life is missing. Sound familiar? Every person to ever walk the planet has felt this way at some point in his or her life.

Now that we have an idea of what emptiness feels like, we can carry our analysis a step further and derive a preliminary definition of emptiness.

When we feel the lack or absence of something, we feel the want of, or the need for, that which we lack. To experience boredom is to experience the need for activity. To experience curiosity is to experience the need for understanding. To experience loneliness is to experience the need for love.

The lack of and the need for something go hand-in-hand. They are two ways of describing the same feeling. Thus, we can say that *emptiness is the need for fulfillment.*

This definition is straightforward and probably not too hard to accept. In deference to Aristotle, we could say that it is self-evident. Solid though it may be, however, our preliminary definition of emptiness is also limited. Before we can use it to help us explore the universe's state of origin and to help us develop a theoretical construct that will allow us to explain how the world we know could have come about from that state, we need to expand on it. To continue our analysis, our experience of emptiness has an essential nature, *consciousness*, which demonstrates two facets: *motivation* and *uncertainty*.

Emptiness is not something we perceive as the result of input from our eyes, ears, or other physical senses. We experience emptiness as an inner awareness, as an internal state of being. We feel boredom. We feel curiosity. We feel loneliness. Emptiness exists as an inner sensation. It is the way we are at times. Emptiness is the state of needing fulfillment. Emptiness is the awareness, or consciousness, of emptiness.

Inherent within our consciousness of emptiness is motivation. To experience the need for something is to at the same time experience the urge to fulfill that need. With boredom comes the drive to create activity. With curiosity comes the drive to create understanding. With loneliness comes the drive to create love. To feel emptiness is to feel a tug on one's being—the energy to grow, to build, to move on. With emptiness, there comes the motivation to create fulfillment.

Inherent within our consciousness of emptiness is also uncertainty. To experience the need for something is to feel concern as to how to fulfill that need. With boredom comes the question, how to create activity. With curiosity comes the question, how to create understanding. With loneliness comes the question, how to create love. Uncertainty produces the trial and error of life, for without the element of the unknown we could satisfy our every need the instant we felt it. With emptiness, there exists uncertainty as to how to create fulfillment.

Based on the above analysis, we can put forth the following general and more useful definition of emptiness:

> Emptiness is the *consciousness* of the need to create fulfillment and thus of the *motivation* to create fulfillment and of the *uncertainty*, or potential uncertainty, as to how to create fulfillment.

I realize that the concept of emptiness as presented here, self-evident though it may be, is new to many readers. I also realize that the process we used to derive it is less rigorous than the reader may be accustomed. Remember, we are dealing with the universe at a point in its evolution not associated with a physical expression and thus one that does not lend itself to a quantified approach. In regard to the above points, I ask that for the time being you accept the definition of emptiness as stated and trust me to further develop it in later chapters. When we set aside the idea that consciousness is the result of an evolution of matter and, as we have begun to do, explore the possibility that matter emerged from and reflects an underlying evolution of consciousness, we make possible a remarkable synthesis of ideas. As if our humble definition of emptiness was the theoretical kingpin, the many disjointed and ostensibly irreconcilable views that comprise our present understanding of the universe and its evolution seemingly fall into their proper place. So natural does this synthesis occur, and so explanatory the account of the universe that emerges from it, that when it comes to our notion of emptiness, one cannot but believe to have come upon some fundamental quality of nature.

With this point, we return to the chapter's premise. Deduction led us to the possibility that the universe began in the simplest state imaginable, the only state that nothing could have come before—the state of emptiness. Based on our knowledge of emptiness, what now can we infer about the universe's state of origin?

If, as the logic of our argument suggests, the universe began as emptiness, and if, as I promise, our definition of emptiness holds true, we are drawn to the conclusion that the universe began as a state of consciousness. But this consciousness would be far more primitive than our own awareness or of any in our modern experience. Based on traditional notions of the divine, it would also be far more primitive than any we associate with a god or Supreme Being. It would be the least complex state of awareness there ever was—the simplest state imaginable. Our analysis suggests that, at its origin—or, as Teilhard characterized it, at its "alpha" point—the universe existed as an elemental sense of void, as a rudimentary feeling of want, as a fundamental discernment of motivation and of impending uncertainty. The universe existed in a state of potential. The universe began as emptiness. At its beginning, the universe felt the need to create fulfillment.

PART ONE

Emergence

2

Perception

A T A MOMENT IN time cosmologists estimate to have taken place approximately fifteen billion years ago, the earliest manifestation of our physical universe came into existence. In this and the next two chapters, we look at the emergence of time and space and relate this emergence to an underlying evolution of consciousness. Specifically, we focus on the process through which such internal and external transformation could have taken place. With respect to the familiar big bang scenario of cosmic formation, one can think of the next three chapters as addressing the point in creation when time equaled zero and the interval that immediately followed when the laws of physics as we presently understand them have yet to come into play. The first part of the book concludes when our depiction of evolution reaches the point where the universe marks a key turning point and attains the form that will allow it to advance into its second major evolutionary period, that of structure. I call this threshold *Autonomy in Unity*.

In the last chapter, we put forth the idea that the universe began in the simplest state imaginable, the only state that nothing could have come before—the state of emptiness. We defined emptiness and then, based on our definition, concluded that the universe began as a rudimentary consciousness, as a primordial awareness of want, motivation, and potential uncertainty. The universe felt the need to create fulfillment.

This brings us to the questions that form the basis of the first part of the book: What are time and space? How could they have emerged from the universe's primordial state of need? And through what theoretical mechanism can we unify internal and external? Before we delve into these and other issues, however, I would like to touch on a preliminary point. Many people find it difficult to understand the idea of emptiness as it applies to the universe's origin. For this reason, I would like to look more closely at the concept and to offer a suggestion that may make it easier to work with as the book progresses.

In our attempt to understand emptiness as the state of consciousness that gave rise to the universe, it is only natural to relate this state of being to the levels of awareness familiar to us, namely to the consciousness we associate with life and, in particular, to our own awareness. We may also relate it to the consciousness we associate with a god or Supreme Being.

The universe today exists some fifteen billion years removed in time from the universe at its origin. The present is—as the present can only be—the pinnacle of evolution. It is the point on top of an expanding cone. It is the summit of the evolutionary peak, uplifted by the strata of all prior time.

Countless evolutionary advances have shaped the consciousness we associate with life. In our normal experience, we associate this consciousness with a discrete organic body, with sensitivity to surroundings and, in the case of human awareness, with an ability to reflect and contemplate. Similarly, even though there are many concepts of God, most who accept the existence of a divine entity believe that God's awareness is in some way greater than our own. This is not to deny the existence of a god. Any complete view of the universe such as that to which we aspire must embrace spiritual experience. Rather, it is to say that the level of consciousness we associate with a god or creator differs from the level we associate with the universe's primordial state of emptiness. The forms of consciousness we know today, divine or otherwise, are further removed from that which we propose as the universe's state of origin than, in terms of complexity, the human brain is removed from the subatomic particle.

We relied on our personal experience of emptiness to help us derive a definition of that state—a technique we will use to help us understand other ideas as well. But for us to apply that definition, for us to picture the universe as emptiness—as an awareness not associated with a physical body, as an awareness more primitive, more elementary, more fundamental than any we know firsthand—we must distance ourselves from our experience. We must set aside our ideas of what consciousness is or, in the case of a god, what it could be, for they belong to the present. They belong on the summit of the evolutionary peak.

We must free our minds to journey down the flanks, to flow down the contours until we reach the base. We must imagine a state of awareness absent from external sensation, free from intuition, empty of contemplation—nothing more than the most elementary sense of void. Such is no simple task, but there is a way to approach the problem that may make it easier.

When considering the universe's primordial state of awareness, perhaps it is best to think of it in terms not directly related to consciousness. It may be best to think of it as a mathematical property, as the base unit of awareness. We can go so far as to assign it a value, the number "one," for example. This approach is not a perfect solution to a challenging problem, but as our analysis progresses its usefulness will become apparent. If one is accustomed to dealing with the world in a quantified way or aspires to develop a rigorous interpretation of certain ideas presented in this book, such a step is essential. In any event, as the chapters progress and the idea of the universe beginning as a state of emptiness becomes familiar, the notion will become easier to fathom, perhaps even seem evident.

With this thought, we are ready to move beyond the concept of emptiness and set forth in the direction that will make it possible for us to put it to use. To reach the point where we can do so, we need to introduce three related ideas, the central notions that along with emptiness form the foundation on which we will construct our account of the universe. They are one, *fulfillment*; two, *object*; and, three, the idea that unites these concepts with that of emptiness and allows us to bridge the gap between external and internal, *perception*.

We can think of the first of these notions, "fulfillment," as the antithesis of emptiness. Like emptiness, we can know and understand fulfillment through simple analysis and exploration of inner feeling. What, then, does fulfillment feel like?

There are of course many ideas of fulfillment, but they share a common theme. The notion of fulfillment brings to mind a state of contentment. Some may describe this state as bliss; others may describe it as mystical perfection or as oneness with God or the cosmos. Most of us think of it in terms that are more down-to-earth. At times, we all feel that life is as we want it to be. We all have those moments—rare and fleeting though they almost certainly are—where everything is where it belongs.

Similarly, we often associate the notion of fulfillment with the experience of love. We have all felt, or at least dreamed of, that ultimate union with another; we have all longed for—and those most fortunate have achieved—that feeling of strength and sense of belonging that comes when one devotes one's life to another only to discover that through such sacrifice of self one gains a greater sense of freedom and individuality.

Whatever words we use to describe it, fulfillment, like emptiness, is a state of being. Fulfillment is a form of awareness, the way we are at times, a dimension of consciousness. Fulfillment is the awareness of being fulfilled. When fulfilled, we have no feeling of need or want. We are where we want to be. Consequently, we have no drive to go anywhere else and no uncertainty as to how to get there:

> Fulfillment is the consciousness of need's satisfaction. Absent are want, motivation, and uncertainty.

Simple though this definition may be, it belies an underlying power. This we will come to appreciate in a moment. Next, we need to look at the second of our three additional notions, the idea of "object."

The concept of object is easily understood by way of examples. If we feel the need for something, say to own a car, the object of our need is, simply, the car. If we feel ignorance, or the need to understand, the object of our need is understanding. And, if we feel loneliness, or the need for companionship, the object of our need is, of course, a companion.

The concept of object is as straightforward as it sounds. Object is the thing we want. It is that which when we obtain it allows for the fulfillment of our need. When acquired, object makes possible the transformation of the experience of emptiness into the experience of fulfillment.

The term "acquired" in the previous sentence brings us to our final point, "perception." In order to fulfill a need, it is not enough to know what the object of our need is and that it exists, we must perceive it to be our own.

If we feel the need to own a car, it is only after we buy the car and are handed the keys that we may perceive the object of our need, the car, as our own and experience the fulfillment of our need. If we feel ignorance, or the need to understand, it is only after we achieve the desired knowledge, say completed the class, that we may perceive the object of our need, understanding, as our own and experience the fulfillment of our need. If we feel loneliness, or the need for companionship, it is only after we befriend another that we may perceive the object of our need, a companion, as our own and experience the fulfillment of our need.

Perception denotes movement, the act of perceiving the object of our need to be our own. By way of this action, we transform the experience of emptiness into the experience of fulfillment.

We now have four concepts at our disposal: emptiness, fulfillment, object, and perception. Emptiness and fulfillment are states of awareness. They are static; they are the consciousness of a certain state of being. Object is a discrete entity in some way removed, or taken to be removed, that when obtained fulfills a need. Perception denotes movement, the act of perceiving. Our four concepts are a way of dealing with consciousness as it would have existed in its initial, simplest state, notions that make it possible for us to work with the idea. Emptiness cannot exist without its converse, fulfillment. Fulfillment cannot exist without its converse, emptiness. As such, there must be the basis to move from one to the other. Our four concepts—as abstract and distant from the tangible universe as they at first appear—are the four shapes of stone that when properly set will allow us to build our account of evolution.

So, let us lay the blocks in place, or at least the first few. To do this, we must once again travel back in time. We must journey beyond the age of human thought, beyond the age of life, and beyond the age of cosmic formation. We must return to the beginning, to where the universe we know today, so vast and diverse, existed as emptiness. If, at the point of its origin, the universe existed in a state of emptiness—and if our notions of emptiness, fulfillment, object, and perception are correct—the universe's evolution could have begun in only one way. A word of caution, do not read too much into the following. It is as simple as it seems.

At the beginning, the universe felt the need to create fulfillment. Associated with the universe's need was the object of that need. That object could take only one form—the only form available, the form that in the most fundamental sense denotes fulfillment itself. Motivated by emptiness—motivated by its need to create fulfillment—the universe turned in on itself and grasped itself in its own awareness. The universe took itself as its own, as an entity of consciousness within itself. The universe perceived itself as the object of its need.

Perception is action, and action manifests in—or more correctly is—time and space. Through what form other than time and space can action exist as or reveal itself through? We can think of the external—time and space—as the movement of the internal—consciousness. The external is our way of relating to and describing the act of perception associated with the internal. And if this is true, what would the external expression, or manifestation, of the universe's original act of perception have looked like? If perception denotes movement, and movement is driven by need, we can picture the external construct that resulted as uniform "energy" that existed as all space.

With this image in mind, we need to gather our thoughts. If one accepts the concepts of emptiness, fulfillment, object, and perception, the idea that the universe perceived itself as the object of its need to create fulfillment reasonably follows. The relationship between internal and external that results is not as straightforward. This relationship is subtle, and we have only begun to explore its intricacies. We have laid the foundation to develop a solid understanding of time and space, but we have yet to achieve the background necessary to do so. Likewise, we must view with caution the picture of the external universe we have created, for we have yet to learn how to interpret it. We live in a world where time appears to flow and objects appear to move through space. Our world obeys physical laws. As previously stated, at this point we are describing the universe at a stage in its evolution where such laws do not apply.

In light of this introspection, let us highlight the evolutionary scenario we have developed to the point where it now stands: *Step one*: the universe existed in a state of emptiness. We can think of this state as a mathematical property—as the universe's initial, or base, level of consciousness. *Step two*: motivated by emptiness, or the need to create fulfillment, the universe turned in on itself and grasped itself in its own awareness; the universe perceived itself as the object of its need. As it did, its action manifested in an external construct we can crudely visualize as uniform energy that existed as all space.

Now, for the *third* and final step of what we will define as the universe's initial *creative cycle*. With the perception of itself as object, the universe's need to create fulfillment stood realized. The universe's consciousness of emptiness became the universe's consciousness of fulfillment. But such is not the attainment of perfection that it may appear, for no sooner had fulfillment begun then it ended. Fulfillment results from perception of object. Perception is driven by need. With fulfillment, need and perception ended. The universe's external manifestation snapped out of existence. The first click of time had passed. Emptiness returned and, for reasons we will explore, felt more empty. The universe no longer existed at its base level of awareness. The universe's need to create fulfillment drove the creation of fulfillment, which led to a greater awareness—to a greater consciousness of the need for fulfillment.

3

Autocatalysis and Uncertainty

IT WOULD BE USEFUL if the pattern of events associated with what we defined as the universe's initial "creative cycle" became second nature to us, at least to some degree. So, at the risk of coming across as repetitive, I would like to begin the chapter with a review of this pattern. *Figure 1* will make this easier.

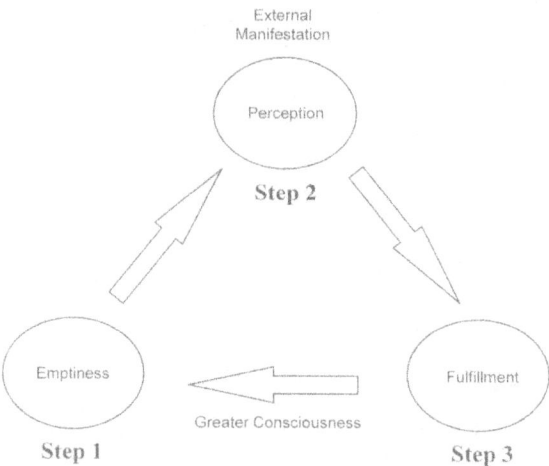

Fig. 1. The Creative Cycle. Step one: the universe existed in a state of emptiness. It felt the need to create fulfillment. Step two: Motivated by its need to create fulfillment, the universe perceived itself as the object of its need, resulting in an external manifestation. Step three: Perception of self as object transformed the experience of emptiness into the experience of fulfillment. This led to an increase in consciousness and to a more intensely felt experience of emptiness.

Step one: The universe existed in a state of emptiness, or felt the need to create fulfillment.

Step two: Motivated by its need to create fulfillment, the universe turned in on itself and grasped itself in its own awareness; the universe perceived itself as the object of its need. As it did, the universe's internal act of perception manifested in an external construct we can describe as uniform energy that existed as all space.

Step three: Perception of self as object transformed the universe's consciousness of emptiness into a consciousness of fulfillment. But with fulfillment, need and, consequently, perception ended. The universe's external manifestation snapped out of existence. The first click of time had passed. The consciousness that was the universe had grown. The universe's experience of emptiness had intensified.

One more time: emptiness drove perception of self as object, which led to external manifestation and fulfillment, which led to a more intense experience of emptiness. It sounds like we ended up in about the same place we started or that we developed the basis for some philosophical computer program stuck in a loop. Such comparisons would be valid if it were not for two factors. The first is the growth, or *autocatalysis*,[1] of consciousness we stated took place during the cycle. The second is the one characteristic of emptiness we have yet to consider, *uncertainty*. As we will see, these factors have the power to propel our emerging model of creation in an entirely new direction.

Before we move on, however, a brief remark about the nature of the material we have found ourselves caught up in and perhaps struggling to understand is in order.

As the reader has no doubt observed, we have begun our inquiry into the nature of the universe on a highly abstract level. Offhand, it is hard to think of less tangible concepts than emptiness, fulfillment, object, and perception. Difficulty arises in that the reason many people read a book like this—and ultimately the reason I wrote one—falls closer to the immediate concerns of life. We are curious about the universe, but only to the extent that increasing our knowledge of it can help us better understand who we are and how, as conscious beings existing within the universe, we can live in a more meaningful way.

I assure you that this deeply personal aim is the underlying objective of this book, as it should be for any book of its type. But we face a dilemma. As we discussed in the preface, to achieve an aim such as ours with the clarity needed for it to be truly revealing, we must take into consideration

---

1. Though it may be apparent in the following discussion, I am using the term "autocatalysis" in the general sense as opposed to the strict sense as it would be used in chemistry. For our purposes, autocatalysis simply means self-induced growth.

a key tenet of Teilhardian philosophy, the notion of *evolutionary context.* To understand ourselves most deeply, we must examine ourselves in the light of everything that came before us; we must see ourselves in the context of the universe's evolution.

Yet, the more removed in time from our own we venture, the more distant we travel from our day-to-day experiences. Consequently, the harder it is for us to relate to what we see and learn. The bottom line, the further from the present we explore, the more abstractly we must conduct our exploration.

So, where does this leave us? On my part, perhaps I can offer little more than a word of assurance. As our depiction of evolution progresses and we draw closer to our own time, we will approach things in a more familiar and personally meaningful way. This is not to say that we can treat the concepts we are now developing lightly. They form the foundation on which we will build the ideas that come. To establish evolutionary context, we must deal with certain issues in an abstract, if not at times a roundabout, manner. If I may be the judge, however, the reward at the end of our journey will far outweigh the journey's challenge.

With this word of encouragement, we return to matters of theoretical consequence and delve into the two ideas that form the basis of this chapter and that will allow us to advance our understanding of evolution: autocatalysis and uncertainty.

As we stated, the universe's initial creative cycle began with it at its base level of awareness and ended with it at a new, higher level of awareness. We can explain this autocatalysis of consciousness in an intuitive way and in an analytical way.

We will start with the first approach and relate the matter to our own lives. We wake up in the morning and go about our daily business, engaging in various actions and undergoing various experiences as we do. We then go to bed at night in some way changed by our actions and experiences. Whether we went to work during the day, attended class, witnessed a crime, or narrowly avoided an auto wreck, we learned something and, though the knowledge we gained may have had no deeper philosophical meaning than not to tailgate when we drive, it left us in some way an older, more seasoned individual. We began the day at one level of consciousness and as a result of our actions and experiences ended the day at a new, higher level of consciousness. Consciousness plus action and experience gives greater consciousness.

This pattern of consciousness growth sounds fine-and-well on the human level, but how can we establish it on the level of the universe's emergence?

To achieve this aim, we begin by denoting the universe's initial, or base, level of consciousness as the figure "C_i," for initial consciousness, and its level of consciousness at the end of its first creative cycle as the figure "C_f," for final consciousness. We will also denote the second step in the cycle as the letter "P" to indicate perception of self as object and the experience of fulfillment. This assignment of terms allows us to describe the creative cycle using the following expression:

$$C_i + P \rightarrow C_f$$

Where: C_i = Initial Consciousness
P = Perception of Self as Object
C_f = Final Consciousness

The universe's initial consciousness of emptiness, C_i, plus the action associated with the perception of itself as object, P, led to a greater consciousness of emptiness, C_f.

With the process now expressed in a form that we can easily work with, we need to take a closer look at the second step in the cycle. By perception of self as object, we are saying that the universe embraced itself in its own awareness. We are making the statement that the universe incorporated its initial level of consciousness within itself. This incorporation of consciousness allows us to associate the second step in the cycle with a level of consciousness that from a theoretical standpoint is equal to that of the universe's initial level of consciousness. Or, in terms of consciousness, we can state that P is equivalent to C_i and rewrite the above expression as follows:

$$C_i + C_i \rightarrow C_f \qquad \text{Given: } P \equiv C_i$$

From here, it is a matter of simple algebra to assign a value to C_i and complete the argument as to how a growth in consciousness could have taken place:

$$1C_i + 1C_i \rightarrow C_f = 2C_i$$

Initial consciousness plus the perception of self as object led to the experience of fulfillment, which led to a consciousness of emptiness twice as intense. Consciousness plus perception of self as object gives greater consciousness.

Like the idea of the universe beginning in a state of emptiness, the idea of self, or "auto," catalysis of consciousness takes a little time to get used to. We are accustomed to thinking of consciousness in terms of life. Consequently, when we approach the concept of its growth on a more fundamental level—in this case from at the bottom of the evolutionary peak—we need to work with it to appreciate its significance. As we gain this experience though, I think you will find the idea fundamental.

This brings us to the notion of uncertainty. With the universe's inability to sustain its experience of fulfillment—with the universe's greater consciousness of emptiness—there arose a degree of uncertainty as to how to create fulfillment.

The idea of uncertainty is intuitive. For this reason, a simple analogy will suffice to introduce us to the concept. Once again, we will draw on the human level to make our comparison.

Imagine you are a construction worker and your boss gives you the job to knock down a concrete wall. Now also imagine that your boss is not the brightest guy on the planet and he hands you a rubber mallet to do the job.

You walk up to the wall, get a good grip on your rubber mallet, and let fly with a vicious blow. The mallet, of course, bounces off the wall without damaging it. Now imagine that, like your boss, you are not the brightest person in the world, and you decide to hit the wall again. Because your first blow had no effect, you will invariably feel a degree of uncertainty as to the outcome produced by your second blow.

Likewise, if you were to continue to hit the wall, so long as your blows had no effect, each strike would increase your uncertainty as to the outcome yielded by the next. Stated generally:

> The inability of an action to produce or to sustain a desired outcome increases the uncertainty as to the outcome created by a repeat of the action.

At the end of the universe's initial creative cycle, uncertainty no longer existed in potential. The universe's greater need to create fulfillment was mitigated by a degree of uncertainty as to how to create fulfillment.

This completes our introduction to the concepts of uncertainty and autocatalysis of consciousness. To grasp the significance of these ideas, we need to move beyond definitions and see how our concepts tie in with the creative cycle. So, once again, we return to the time of the universe's emergence and continue our depiction of evolution.

We left off with the universe at the end of its first creative cycle. At that point, the universe existed as a consciousness of emptiness that at least theoretically was twice as great as its original level. This state of awareness consisted of two facets. Most of the experience of emptiness was felt as the motivation to create fulfillment. A fraction, however, was felt as the uncertainty as to how to create fulfillment:

$$C_i + P \rightarrow C_m + C_u$$

Where: C_i = Initial Consciousness
P = Perception of Self as Object
C_m = Consciousness of Motivation
C_u = Consciousness of Uncertainty

Driven by a now greater experience of the need to create fulfillment, the creative cycle repeated. Once again, the universe perceived itself as the object of its need. This time, greater motivation led to greater perception of self as object, which led to greater external manifestation and to a more intense experience of fulfillment. Once again, with fulfillment, need and consequently perception ended, and the universe's external manifestation snapped out of existence. The second click of time had passed. Emptiness returned and felt emptier. Consciousness had grown—and so had uncertainty.

Here, the reader may be intrigued by what appears to be a philosophical dilemma. How can the universe's experience of emptiness and fulfillment increase? Was not the universe's original state of emptiness as empty as it gets? Is not any experience of fulfillment completely fulfilling? We must realize that emptiness and fulfillment do not change. Our definitions remain true. The consciousness that experiences these states of being changes. The universe attained a greater level of awareness with the completion of its first then second creative cycle, and thus was able to experience emptiness and fulfillment in a successively more evolved way.

Cycle after cycle, the process repeated. Driven by increased need, the universe perceived itself as the object of its need with increased motivation. Greater perception created greater external manifestation and a more intense experience of fulfillment. But with each experience of fulfillment, need and perception ended. Emptiness returned, and uncertainty grew. Cycle after cycle, the clicks of time passed. The universe's external construct snapped into and out of existence. The universe's consciousness of emptiness grew, but the portion felt as the motivation to create fulfillment increased at a decreasing rate while the portion felt as uncertainty increased at an increasing rate and thus occupied a larger part of the total:

$$C_i + P \rightarrow \uparrow C_m + \uparrow C_u$$

Where: C_i = Initial Consciousness
P = Perception of Self as Object
C_m = Consciousness of Motivation
C_u = Consciousness of Uncertainty

Figure 2 will further help to clarify the relationship between motivation and uncertainty. The bars represent five hypothetical creative cycles. The height of each bar shows the universe's total consciousness of emptiness. The lighter area shows the portion felt as motivation. Because the level of motivation is directly proportional to the strength of perception, which is directly proportional to the intensity of fulfillment and to the degree of external manifestation, this area also represents the level of these factors. The dark area at the bottom of the last four bars shows uncertainty. With each cycle, motivation, perception, fulfillment, and external manifestation increase but, because uncertainty occupies a larger part of the universe's total experience of emptiness, at a decreasing rate.

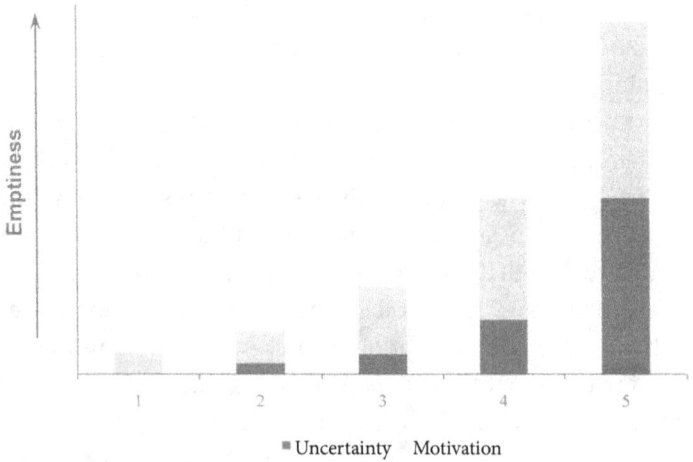

■ Uncertainty   Motivation

Fig. 2. The First Five Creative Cycles. The height of each bar shows the universe's total consciousness of emptiness. The light area shows the portion felt as motivation. The dark area shows the portion felt as uncertainty. With each cycle, motivation increased but, because uncertainty occupied more of the total consciousness of emptiness, at a decreasing rate.

If you are thinking that the trend of increasing uncertainty with respect to motivation has to lead somewhere, you are right. But before we go any further, it would be useful to refocus our eyes and look at the universe's creative cycles from an external point of view.

In our emerging theory of evolution, each act of perception denotes one click of time. Flow of time can be understood as the effect created by successive clicks of time. Likewise, each act of perception marks the rebirth of the spatial quality of the universe's external construct at a new, more evolved level.

This is somewhat analogous to the way a motion picture film projects a moving image. A filmstrip consists of a series of individual photos, or frames, that when viewed sequentially create the effect of a moving picture. We can think of the snap of each frame in front of the projector's lamp as one click of time and the projection of each frame's image on the screen as one rebirth of space. Like the screening of a motion picture, the individual acts of perception that occur with each creative cycle produce an external manifestation with a temporal and a spatial quality—they create the effect of time flow and space transformation.

This simple pattern of one creative cycle to one click of time and one rebirth of space forms the basis of the model of external manifestation we will be using. But it has certain limitations that encourage us to look deeper.

We must realize that even though it is convenient to think of time and space as separate qualities—and we will do so on occasion—they are not. We cannot separate the universe's spatial manifestation from its click of time. The universe's external construct exists as the manifestation of an underlying act of perception. The external is not time and space; but, as Einstein recognized a century ago; it is *time-space*.[2]

To make matters more intriguing, the universe's external construct has a "contradictory" nature. The creative cycle has three steps: one, emptiness; two, perception and external manifestation; and, three, fulfillment leading to greater emptiness. External manifestation is associated with the second step, with the act of perception. Emptiness and fulfillment exist as states of awareness; they have no expression in time and space.

On one hand, this solves a nagging problem. When pondering the universe's origin, we may be tempted to ask what came before the original

---

2. Einstein generally used the term space-time.

state of emptiness. The answer is that the question makes no sense. Prior to the universe's first act of perception there was no before and no place for anything to be.

On the other hand, the internal nature of emptiness and fulfillment creates what on first inquiry appears to be a philosophical quandary. In the creative cycle, an internal state of emptiness and fulfillment coincides with, or to make it easier to visualize, separates each act of perception and its corresponding event of time-space manifestation. From a purely external point of view, however, nothing reveals itself to delineate one manifestation from another. Unlike in the motion picture film where a brief interval of time separates the image projected by each frame, in the creative cycle each event of external manifestation butts against the next.

This leads us to the conclusion that the external universe has opposing natures. Time and space change in units while at the same time they change in an unbroken flow.

This apparent contradiction will be familiar to the physicist accustomed to dealing with the wave-particle characteristic of matter. If we do an experiment to study light as a wave, it will appear to us as a wave. If we do an experiment to study light as a particle, it will appear to us as a particle, a photon. For our present purpose, it is enough to be aware of the conflicting nature of the external and to realize that it is a dilemma we create. It is a contradiction of nature that results when we impose an external view on what is fundamentally an internal process. Yet, this is not to say that an external view does not have certain advantages, not the least of which is that it can help us create the visual image we need to bring the chapter into focus.

If we picture the external manifestation that resulted from the universe's first creative cycle as uniform energy that existed as all space, we can picture the external manifestation that resulted from subsequent creative cycles as a sequence of such emanations of uniform energy. Each emanation would coincide with one rebirth of space, and since consciousness grew and perception increased in strength with each cycle, each spatial emanation would be more intense than the one before. This intensification, however, would not take the form of increased brightness. Brightness implies density, which implies a particulate as opposed to a uniform nature. Intensification would reveal itself in a more fundamental way—as an increase in the size of space with respect to the previous event of external manifestation.

Here we come to another limitation in our "film and projector" view of time and space. When we speak of space and uniform energy, we are not talking about uniform energy occupying space. Space and uniform energy would be one-and-the-same. When viewed over time—over the course of successive creative cycles—we can picture the universe's external emergence at this stage in evolution as uniform energy that existed as all of expanding space.

But, like the movement of consciousness that underlies it, this expansion of time-space was not without its outcome. Cycle after cycle, emptiness, perception, and fulfillment increased. Time clicked; space and uniform energy expanded. Then the universe's internal and external expansion approached its end. With each cycle, more of the universe's experience of emptiness was felt as uncertainty and less was felt as the motivation to drive the next cycle. Consciousness, perception, and fulfillment increased, but at a decreasing rate. Finally, the universe reached the point where it exhausted its potential to create fulfillment through simple perception of itself as the object of its need. As *Figure 3* shows, uncertainty grew to the level where it occupied the entire experience of emptiness. Uncertainty reached the point where it overwhelmed.

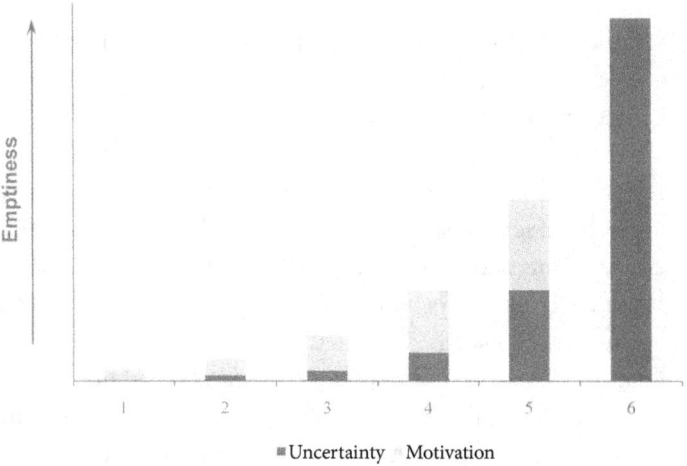

Fig. 3. Uncertainty Overwhelms. The bars illustrate the increase in uncertainty that took place over the course of five hypothetical creative cycles, to climax at the point where in the sixth cycle uncertainty occupied the universe's entire consciousness of emptiness.

4

Autonomy in Unity

IN THE LAST CHAPTER, we left off with the universe at what we can characterize as a transition point in its evolution. Uncertainty had grown to the level where it occupied the entire experience of emptiness:

$$C_i + P \rightarrow C_u$$

Where: C_i = Initial Consciousness
P = Perception of Self as Object
C_u = Consciousness of Uncertainty

As a result, the universe no longer felt the motivation to engage in an additional creative cycle. But as uncertainty reached the point where it overwhelmed, it also reached the point that made imminent its own collapse and the emergence of an entirely new evolutionary direction.

To understand this, recall that each creative cycle gave rise to a growth in the universe's consciousness, and that this consciousness could be experienced as motivation or uncertainty. Another way to look at this is that, with each cycle, uncertainty locked up, or held in potential, the motivational aspect of a vastly amplified experience of emptiness. But, as *Figure 4* illustrates, this locking up of energy was not without its outcome. Shown by the last two bars in the figure, when uncertainty reached the point where it locked up the universe's entire experience of emptiness, the failure of the universe's present evolutionary approach became certain and uncertainty collapsed.

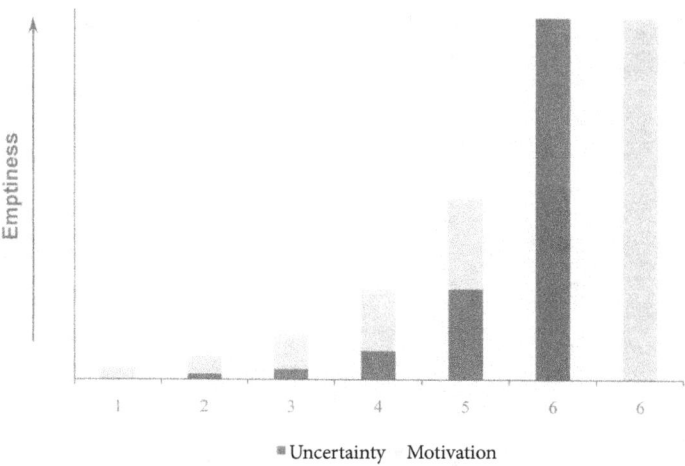

■ Uncertainty   Motivation

Fig. 4. Uncertainty Collapses. When uncertainty reached the point where it oc-cupied the universe's entire consciousness of emptiness, the exhaustion of the universe's present evolutionary level became certain and uncertainty collapsed. This is shown by the second bar associated with the sixth cycle.

Recall our construction worker. Each time the man struck the con-crete wall with his rubber mallet, the uncertainty he felt as to whether his next blow would damage the wall increased. If the man were to con-tinue to hit the wall, his uncertainty would eventually overcome his will to strike another blow. He would recognize the futility of his action and no longer feel uncertain about it. At the cycle where uncertainty over-whelmed, the obsolescence of the universe's present evolutionary direc-tion was no longer in doubt. It became certain that the universe could not continue to create fulfillment through simple perception of itself as the object of its need; and, with this certainty, uncertainty ended and the universe's entire consciousness of emptiness was felt as the motivation to create fulfillment:

$$C_i + P \rightarrow C_m$$ Where: C_i = Initial Consciousness
P = Perception of Self as Object
C_m = Consciousness of Motivation

This motivation not only drove the universe to perceive itself as the object of its need to create fulfillment but to do so in a new way. This moti-vation lifted the universe out of its past evolutionary direction and thrust it into a new evolutionary direction. As *Figure 5* shows, the universe had created the consciousness to pursue a new strategy of evolution—to cross a *threshold* to a new level of evolutionary advance.

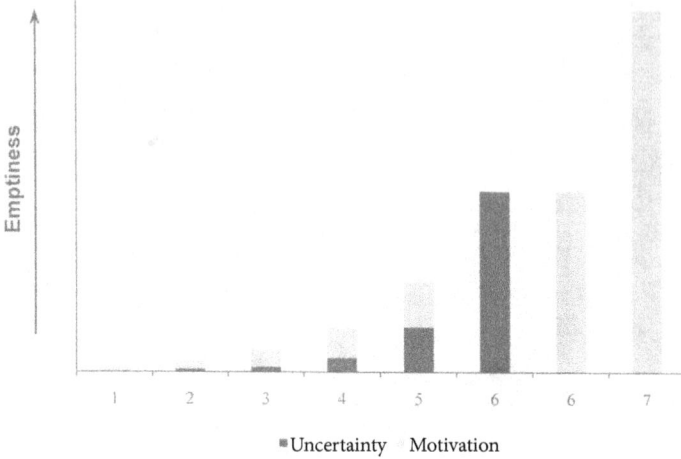

Fig. 5. A Threshold is Crossed. With the collapse of uncertainty, the universe's entire consciousness of emptiness was felt as the motivation to create fulfillment. This motivation lifted the universe across the threshold to a new evolutionary level. Shown here with the seventh creative cycle.

Symbolically, the threshold would look like this:

$$C_i + P \rightarrow C_u \rightarrow C_m$$

Where:

C_i = Initial Consciousness
P = Perception of Self as Object
C_m = Consciousness of Motivation
C_u = Consciousness of Uncertainty

Which leads to a new series of creative cycles on a new evolutionary level:

$$C_i + P \rightarrow C_u \rightarrow C_m \qquad \Longrightarrow \qquad C_i + P \rightarrow {\uparrow}C_m + {\uparrow}C_u$$

For the mathematically inclined, if we let the symbol "()" represent the feedback loop between cycles, the following expression would represent the repetition of creative cycles that leads to the crossing of the universe's first creative threshold:

$$\begin{array}{l} {}^{1}_{0} \boxed{} \to \; () \; C_i + P \to \uparrow C_m + \uparrow C_u \end{array}$$

If we let the symbol "[" represent the threshold we can further simplify the expression:[1]

$$ {}^{1}_{0} \; [\; () \; C_i + P \to \uparrow C_m + \uparrow C_u $$

Which takes us beyond the idea of the evolutionary threshold to the nature of the universe's new level of evolutionary advance. For the reason that at such an early stage in evolution there was no other avenue to pursue, the universe could progress in only one evolutionary direction. There was only one evolutionary road to follow.

The universe not only grasped itself as an entity of consciousness within itself, as it had done before, it grasped itself as grasping itself. The universe not only perceived itself as the object of its need to create fulfillment, it perceived itself as perceiving itself.

An external construct manifested. But we can no longer picture this external construct as uniform energy that existed as all space. Due to the universe's enwrapping of perception, due to the universe not only perceiving itself as an entity of consciousness within itself but to it perceiving *itself* as perceiving *itself* as this entity, we can visualize this external manifestation as two areas of uniform energy that together existed as all space. The universe's nesting of a secondary act of perception within its overall act of perception, manifested as a doubling of space to form two identical regions of uniform energy.

Cycle after cycle, the process repeated. During the universe's second cycle at this evolutionary level, it enwrapped the more complex degree of perception it had become to grasp itself as four entities of consciousness within itself. During its third cycle, it enwrapped this still more complex

1. The following mathematical expression denotes the repetition of the creative cycle up to the universe's first evolutionary threshold. If one is inclined to symbolically express the creative mechanism, it can be adapted to higher evolutionary levels or to nestled evolutionary levels.

degree of perception to grasp itself as eight entities of consciousness within itself. During its third cycle, it enwrapped this level of perception to grasp itself as sixteen entities of consciousness within itself. With each cycle, complexity and consciousness multiplied.

This introduces a new dimension into our analysis, one that the physicist who deals with the early stages of cosmic formation will find intriguing and that for us will become important in the book's next section. Because each entity of consciousness was a perceptual reproduction of the first, each would be identical, each would have the same level of awareness. Because each entity had the same level of awareness and because the number of entities always doubled with each cycle, the decrease in motivation that occurred as a result of an increase in uncertainty had to reveal itself other than by a change in these factors. Like other events early in evolution, the simplicity of the universe leads us to conclude that this development could take only one form.

Increasing uncertainty and decreasing strength of perception revealed itself as a weakening in the relationship between each "doubling of entities" and overall consciousness. As uncertainty increased, the universe less tightly embraced each doubling of entities. The universe not only consisted of entities of consciousness but of entities in a perceptual relationship to overall consciousness. This internal organization would have an external manifestation, and it is here that we can glimpse its form.

Just as internally each cycle resulted in a doubling of entities of consciousness, externally each cycle resulted in a doubling of regions of uniform energy. If we consider each doubling of regions to be a group, external organization would take physical form as a scattering of regions of uniform energy within each group, wrapped within a scattering of the groups themselves. Old groups and regions would be more tightly aligned than new groups and regions. Here our view of the universe faces a familiar difficulty. The regions of uniform energy did not occupy a larger space, like marbles in a jar, but represented space itself. The scattering of groups and regions was not a fabric of entities woven in space, but a fabric of space.

The cosmologist will appreciate this image of the early universe in that it offers a theoretical basis for an accepted but not well understood characteristic of cosmic formation, the differentiation of time-space. At some point in the universe's formation, time-space jumped from uniformity to differentiation, otherwise we would not have ended up with stars and planets and be around to consider the matter. Our internal view accounts for this jump in a basic way and, in agreement with thought and observation, suggests that it took place early in the universe's formation. As with all aspects of cosmic emergence, the external reflects the internal.

In general, then, with each repetition of the creative cycle, the universe enwrapped its previous degree of perception. Internally, the universe existed as an entity of consciousness whose growth took place by a doubling of the number of entities of lesser consciousness wrapped within. Externally, the universe existed as a fabric of time-space whose growth took place by a doubling of the number of regions of uniform energy organized within the whole. But, as at the universe's previous evolutionary level, the cyclic growth of uncertainty would assure that this internal and external advancement was not without its limit.

Before we bring this scenario to its conclusion and wrap up the chapter and our section on the universe's emergence, it would be useful to backtrack somewhat. This is a good time to give our minds a breather and put the first part of the book in perspective.

As you may recall from the preface, Teilhardian philosophy is founded on four principles: The first is the conviction that we can understand the universe's fundamental nature and purpose. The second is the idea of the universe as an evolution, the notion that the universe is a process of becoming. The third is the idea of evolutionary context, the notion that to understand a particular moment in evolution we must examine that moment in light of the evolution that led up to it. The forth is the idea of intrinsic consciousness, the notion that consciousness is not the result of the organization of matter, present only in life, but that it underlies all levels of external organization.

When we set forth to explore the universe's emergence from this "evolution of consciousness" point of view, we are drawn to a particular depiction of events. Our shift in perspective from one that is external to one that includes the universe's internal dimension leads to the unfolding of a specific vision of the early universe and its evolution.

This vision begins with the universe in a state of emptiness and progresses as the universe evolves by way of a process of creative cycles and thresholds. From an internal point of view, we have looked at how this process advanced the universe through two evolutionary stages. The first stage was defined by the universe's perception of itself as the object of its need to create fulfillment. The second stage was defined by the universe's enwrapping of perception to create a doubling of the fundamental entity of consciousness from which it was formerly composed. Externally, this transformation of consciousness manifested as an expansion of space and uniform energy followed by a doubling of the region of space and uniform energy that resulted to form a differentiated time-space fabric that reflected internal organization.

Taken as a whole, we see evolution as the process whereby the universe overcomes uncertainty to recreate itself in states of successively higher consciousness. The fundamental force behind this evolution is emptiness, or the need to create fulfillment. The fundamental aim is the creation of a more conscious, highly evolved experience of fulfillment.

At this point, we have also established the background to summarize our thoughts about key aspects of our evolutionary model. In our theory of evolution, one click of time and one rebirth of space occur with each act of perception, or more generally with each creative cycle. Likewise, we see flow of time and transformation of space to be the result of subsequent acts of perception, or of subsequent creative cycles. As we mentioned, the energy behind this creative activity is emptiness—the need, and thus the motivation, to create fulfillment. Finally, we have reached the point where it is appropriate to name the process whereby time, space, energy, and uncertainty come into play. For reasons that I think are apparent, we will call the pattern of creative cycles and thresholds that we have defined the *creative process*.

One additional point. During the first part of the book, we introduced several ideas by relating them to human experiences. These ideas included emptiness, fulfillment, object, perception, uncertainty, and autocatalysis of consciousness. To do this may seem odd, even at this point. How can we equate the human level with that of the universe at such an early stage in its evolution, or for that matter with that of the universe at all? But if we are dealing with the universe in a way that models its fundamental nature, how can such links between past and present not exist? If we were to disregard such comparisons, would we not be setting ourselves apart from the universe?

With these thoughts, we will return to the creative process and complete the scenario associated with the universe's second evolutionary level. Cycle after cycle, emptiness, perception, and fulfillment increased.

Entities of consciousness doubled and doubled again. Time clicked and space expanded and differentiated. Then the universe's internal and external expansion by the doubling of its previous form approached its end. With each cycle, more of the universe's experience of emptiness was felt as uncertainty, and less was felt as the motivation needed to drive the next cycle. Consciousness, perception, and fulfillment increased, but at a decreasing rate. Then the universe reached the point where it exhausted its potential to create fulfillment through simple enwrapping of perception. Uncertainty grew to overwhelm.

The universe stood on its second evolutionary threshold. But the moment uncertainty overwhelmed, the end of the universe's evolutionary direction was no longer in doubt. Uncertainty collapsed, and the full force of the universe's yet more amplified experience of emptiness released to be felt as the motivation to create fulfillment. This motivation lifted the universe to a new evolutionary level, to the form that would allow it to enter its next major evolutionary period. The universe turned in on itself and grasped itself as what it had become. Externally, the universe existed as an entity made-up of regions of uniform energy organized to form a larger fabric of time-space. Internally, the universe existed as an entity poised for the development of *Structure*—an entity made-up of autonomous entities of consciousness embraced within the consciousness of the whole. The universe crossed the threshold of *autonomy in unity*.

PART TWO

Structure

5

Relationships

IN OUR EXPANDING DEPICTION of evolution, the universe advanced from the time of its emergence, in the neighborhood of fifteen billion years ago, to about four billion years ago by way of the evolution of its internal structure. In this and the next two chapters, we look at this *complexification* of consciousness and relate it to atomic, molecular, and cosmic formation. We also expand our understanding of time, space, and the creative process and reconcile our evolution of consciousness account of the universe to the views put forth by present-day science. The second part of the book concludes as our depiction of evolution reaches the point where the universe crosses a key threshold and attains the form that will allow it to advance into its third major evolutionary period, that of life. I call this threshold *Design Over Structure.*

At the onset of the evolutionary period we call structure, the universe existed as a consciousness made-up of autonomous entities of lesser consciousness. By "autonomous," we mean that each entity of lesser consciousness possessed a degree of independence from the whole and from one another. This degree of separateness within overall consciousness, this degree of "self" within the unity of the universe defined their existence. It also made possible a new evolutionary direction. Motivated by the need to create fulfillment, the cycles of the creative process lifted the universe to greater awareness and complexity through the formation of *relationships* between the autonomous entities of consciousness from which it was composed.

To see how this worked, we begin by introducing an idea called *structure of perception.* As you may recall from the last chapter and our discussion on the universe's previous evolutionary stage, the growth of uncertainty and the weakening strength of perception that resulted with each doubling of consciousness created an arrangement of entities within overall consciousness, "a scattering of entities in a group, wrapped within a scattering of groups." More to the point, the entities of consciousness that made-up the universe were held in a relationship to one another and the whole by an intricate web, or wrap, of perception. We can think of this web or wrap as a framework, as a structure of perception.

Any structure of perception, simple though it may be, implies a level of consciousness, or the awareness through which the components that make up the structure maintain their relationship. Thus, on crossing the threshold of autonomy in unity, the universe consisted of two divisions. A portion of its consciousness was attributable to the entities from which it was composed, and a portion was attributable to the organization of these entities—to the structure of perception through which they were related and that was available when uncertainty collapsed.

From this, it follows that the universe's awareness would be greater than the sum consciousness of its component entities. The whole is greater than the sum of its parts. It also follows that the awareness experienced by the individual entity would be greater than the level it would experience if alone. To exist as an autonomous entity of consciousness, the component entity would have to be in some rudimentary way aware of overall consciousness and of its place in the structure of that consciousness. The component entity would have to be in some rudimentary way aware of the universe's emptiness, of its need to create fulfillment.

Given these observations, the universe could advance to greater consciousness in two ways: by increasing the awareness of its component entities and by increasing the complexity of the structure of perception through which they were arranged. It accomplished these objectives by creating relationships. Cycle after cycle, the universe perceived itself as the object of its need to create fulfillment. As it did, the entities of consciousness from which it was composed perceived one another as the object of their need to create fulfillment. The entities of consciousness that made-up the greater consciousness that was the universe created mutually fulfilling relationships sustained by the power of their need through local creative cycles.

When we look at the relationship in this way, its origin seems inescapable. If during the universe's first evolutionary period the universe advanced through simple perception of itself as object, and during its second evolutionary period it advanced through the formation of conscious entities within itself, it stands to reason that it would next organize these entities. The most remarkable qualities about evolution on this level lie in this organization. What can we say about the relationship?

As we mentioned, the relationship would generate its own creative cycles and structure of perception. Consequently, the characteristics we associate with the creative cycle and with a structure of perception would exist in the relationship. Specifically, the consciousness of the relationship would be greater than the sum awareness of its component entities, and the consciousness experienced by each component entity would be greater than the level it would experience if alone.

When looked at as a whole, therefore, the relationship would be more than an arrangement of components. It would exist as an aspect of consciousness removed from the entities that constituted it being. The relationship would be an item, a distinct entity, an autonomous aspect of consciousness in itself.

Moreover, a component would experience a different level of awareness in a relationship than when not in a relationship. As such, the nature of the component would vary. When in a relationship with one entity, a component would experience a different level of awareness and thus be a different entity than it would when in a relationship with three, or four, or five entities. The nature, or the *identity*, of an entity would be a function of its relationship to other entities.

A related human experience may clarify these points. While attending college in the Northwest United States, I worked summers fighting forest fires. The crews on which I worked numbered about twenty men and women and were often dispatched to fight fires for weeks at a time. During this period, the members of the crew lived and worked in harsh and exhausting conditions and developed a close social relationship. The crew became more than a group of twenty isolated individuals. It gained an identity all its own—a state of existence greater than the sum consciousness of its members. Likewise, being a part of the crew invoked a feeling of belonging and the greater sense of self that results. We were no longer isolated individuals.

The creative nature of the relationship allows us to deduce one additional characteristic, an aspect of the relationship that as our depiction of evolution progresses will reveal much about ourselves. When two or more entities of consciousness perceive one another as the object of their need, the strength of their perception, and the intensity of their experience of fulfillment, would depend on the number of entities in the relationship. The greater the number of entities in a relationship, the more dispersed the individual act of perception. This would lead to a weaker bond between entities and to a less fulfilling relationship. In a relationship composed of two entities, the bond would be stronger and the relationship more fulfilling than in a relationship composed of three, four, or five entities. Consequently, entities in numerically large relationships would be pulled away to form numerically small relationships. This would limit the size, or *collective* tendency, of relationships.[1]

Figure 6 summarizes the characteristics of the relationship. Due to structure of perception, each relationship achieves an autonomous state of being, and each component entity experiences a greater degree of awareness in a relationship than when not in a relationship. This degree of awareness varies with the size of the relationship and leads to entity identity and to the tendency of entities to form small rather than large relationships.

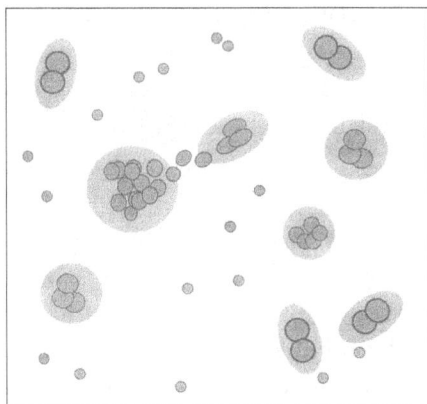

Fig. 6. Relationships. As a result of its structure of perception, each relationship achieved its own autonomous state of being. Each entity within a relationship, in turn, experienced a greater degree of awareness than when not in a relationship. This degree of awareness varied with the size of the relationship and led to entity identity and to the tendency of entities to form small rather than large relationships.

1. Teilhard used the term *collective* to refer to the tendency of conscious entities, human beings in particular, to come together in a way where they draw in on themselves— the twentieth century's growing economic and social interconnectedness of nations, for example. I use the term as it is commonly defined today, to indicate a level of structural complexity. A more collective arrangement is simpler and has more uniform relationships between members: the random distribution of ions, neutrons, and electrons when a gas is in a plasma state. A less collective arrangement is more complex and has more layered, nestled, and interwoven relationships between members. When plasma cools, ions form ionic compounds, electrons are drawn to nuclei to form stable atoms, and atoms come together to form molecules. Marxist societies are said to be more collective. Social structure is uniform, communal, and centrally controlled. Democratic societies are said to be less collective. To a greater extent, members embrace individuality, freedom of thought, and the social foundation of the family.

Another example from the human realm will further bring these ideas home. This time, we will look at a relationship composed of two individuals, a married couple.

Like two entities of consciousness that perceive one another as the object of their need, two individuals in a marriage, or similar arrangement, create a relationship with a state of being of its own. The union between the members—the structure of the marriage—gives the relationship an existence greater than the sum of its members. We often refer to couples simply as the Jones or the Smiths or whoever they may be.

Similarly, the sense of belonging the marriage provides invokes a feeling of security in the individual and a greater sense of self than he or she would experience alone. No person can attain his or her highest state of being adrift in the vacuum of social isolation. As important, with the greater sense of self that the marriage provides, the individual's identity changes. As most who are married will tell you—at least those who will admit it—the relationship alters the way they see and interact with the world. In a broader sense, it changes who they are.

Moreover, an outsider who attempts to encroach into the marriage will tend to be repelled. This is not to say that an outsider could not draw away one partner and cause the marriage to end in divorce, but a marriage has a propensity to limit the number of its members and by doing so to sustain its existence.

In the above example, we are generalizing about human nature and assuming a good marriage. Our point is not to probe too deeply into our make-up at this time but to relate certain ideas about what we call the relationship to a level closer to home.

At the evolutionary stage now of interest to us, we can summarize the outcome of the creative cycles by the trends they established. The universe evolved to greater consciousness as, cycle after cycle, a greater number of component entities perceived one another as the object of their need and by doing so formed relationships. The universe advanced as its structure of perception became more complex and the aspects of consciousness from which it was composed became more autonomous and aware.

What, now, would this complexification of consciousness look like from an external point of view? As was the case during earlier evolutionary stages, each overall creative cycle would mark one click of time and one rebirth of space. Only at this evolutionary level, the external manifestation that took place within this framework is more intriguing.

We can visualize the universe's external evolution over successive creative cycles as a coming together of regions of uniform energy to form clusters of regions. Because these clusters would reflect an underlying relationship, they would exist as autonomous time-space manifestations, as independent entities within the universe's overall time-space fabric. Moreover, from an external vantage, we can characterize the structure of perception that from an internal vantage constituted a relationship as a force or forces, that which holds together the cluster.

With this said, it would be useful to give the fundamental regions of uniform energy that make up a cluster a name. The concept of matter is perhaps premature, but it is appropriate to use a name that will help us introduce the idea in the next chapter. We will call the universe's elemental regions of uniform energy *particles*. But we must remind ourselves that a particle is not an object in time-space but time-space itself. We must visualize the particle as a shadowy figure, as a reflection of internal movement, as a resonance. Here, I think, the physics approach of describing electrons and other subatomic particles in terms of probability density rather than as discrete in space finds its root. As well, we establish the basis for what is popularly called *String Theory*, specifically the fluctuating nature of the universe's elemental constituents.[2]

The idea of the particle and of the cluster of particles as a time-space manifestation becomes more striking when we incorporate two new and particularly appealing ideas into our view of the external. They are *relative time-space* and *accelerating time*.

As we know, an internal relationship exists when two or more entities of consciousness perceive one another as the object of their need to

---

2. In the traditional model of subatomic structure, referred to as the Standard Model, particles called quarks are the building blocks of higher-level particles called hadrons, or particles that like protons and neutrons interact through the strong force. The Standard Model deals with the indecisive nature of a particle that we would attribute to the cyclic nature of the creative process as a probability density. In the alternative String model, of which there are variations, quarks and other indivisible particles are thought of as vibrating strings rather than as particles. The frequency at which a string vibrates—and its sub-vibrations, or mathematical dimensions—determine its type. Frequency implies a cyclic nature that in the evolution of consciousness view we would account for by the creative cycle. Variations in string frequency account for particle types and correspond to our notion of entity identity.

create fulfillment. All the factors we associate with the act of perception, or more generally with the creative cycle, exist on the level of the relationship. Each entity would feel emptiness. Each entity would feel motivation and uncertainty. And each entity would feel fulfillment. Each local creative cycle would also generate an external manifestation. Each local act of perception would create one local click of time and one local rebirth of space. The relationship exists within but autonomous from the universe's overall fabric of time and space—as a time-space fabric relative to its own being.

But our expanded view of the external does not stop here. With each overall creative cycle, a number of local creative cycles could take place. One or more would be associated with each relationship. As the creative process advanced and the number of relationships increased, the number of local creative cycles that took place within each overall creative cycle would also increase. This leads us to a revealing observation and, whereas the idea of relative time-space has been long accepted by physics, with a notion that will be new to many in the field. The greater the number of local acts of perception per overall act of perception, the faster the pace of time—or more precisely the faster the pace of what time as it applies to the universe's overall movement represents, evolution. This does not mean that time as we typically measure it changes, say based on radioactive decay. For reasons that will become apparent as our account of creation advances, radioactive decay unfolds at a constant rate. As the number of relationships increased, time as it relates to the universe's evolution accelerated.

When we take into account the above ideas, our picture of the external universe at this stage in evolution takes on a distinctly chaotic appearance. Over a sequence of spatial rebirths, we see particles unite to form clusters of particles. We see large clusters torn apart to form smaller clusters. We see the type of a particle change as the identity of its associated entity of consciousness changes. Clusters of particles would exist in regions of relative time and space. These regions of relative time and space would change as the clusters changed. Finally, all regions of local external manifestation would exist within an overall fabric of space and accelerating time.

For most of us, the image of the early universe we just described and the concepts on which it is based represent a new way to think about time, space, and cosmic formation. Here a word of reassurance is in order.

Tantalizing though the above view may be it is not necessary to understand it in every detail to achieve the book's objectives. We have touched on the necessary ideas.

What is most important is that we do not lose sight of the overall picture of evolution we have developed, in particular the sequence of major evolutionary stages. Hopefully, if we keep this in mind and add to it as we go, we will be able to advance our understanding of evolution and appreciate its immediate and personal consequences without finding ourselves overwhelmed by its remarkable but less tangible qualities.

Armed with this approach, we will now complete our depiction of the universe's evolutionary level of relationships. Cycle after cycle, emptiness, perception, and fulfillment increased. Time accelerated, and space grew more complex. Then the universe's period of "relationships" approached its end. With each cycle, more of the universe's experience of emptiness was felt as uncertainty and less was felt as the motivation needed to drive the next cycle. The universe reached the point where it exhausted its potential to create fulfillment through the simple formation of relationships. Uncertainty grew to overwhelm.

The universe stood on yet another evolutionary threshold. The greater autonomy and consciousness present within the relationship created the potential for greater perception of object between relationships than between entities alone—and thus greater potential to create fulfillment. Uncertainty collapsed and released the full force of the universe's consciousness of emptiness to be felt as motivation. The universe turned in on itself and grasped itself as what it had become, an entity poised for the development of more complex internal and external structure—an entity defined by the existence of relationships.

6

Atoms, Molecules, and the Cosmos

UP TO THIS POINT in our depiction of evolution, the relatively simple nature of the universe made it possible for us to present a definite scenario of evolutionary events. What else could we expect to have happened during the universe's second evolutionary stage other than a doubling of the fundamental entity of consciousness created during the universe's first evolutionary stage? What else could we expect to have happened during the universe's third evolutionary stage other than the formation of relationships between the entities of consciousness created during the universe's second evolutionary stage? In the period of evolutionary advancement we are about to explore, such specificity is no longer possible or necessary. To understand this, we need to expand our view of the creative process. This will allow us to describe the development of the internal structures that in our evolution of consciousness vision of the universe underlie such familiar external forms as atoms and molecules, stars and galaxies.

To begin with, we need to incorporate several additional ideas into our model of the creative process. I call the first of these ideas *alternative evolutionary directions*. The easiest way to introduce this concept is to use a familiar technique. We will look at the way this aspect of the creative process reveals itself on the human level, or at least at one possible way.

Let us imagine we are engaged in a certain creative activity, say we are writing a story. As most writers will tell you, the drafting of a story, or for that matter of any type of written material, is not a smooth process. We experience periods of clear vision and rapid progress. We experience periods of uncertainty and little progress. And we experience moments of insight.

Driven by the need to tell a story, the writer sets out to compose his work. The first page or two may flow easily, but soon the author questions the story's direction. Eventually, his uncertainty grows to the point where it consumes his entire being. Such is the agony of writing. Like the painter Paul Cézanne, who slashed many of his most ambitious canvases, the author may tear-up his manuscript or curse himself for studying English and not accounting in college. But if he perseveres, his uncertainty will collapse, and he will cross a threshold. The author will experience an insight, and his story will breakthrough to a new level. Such is the joy of writing.

It is this "new level" that is of interest to us, for it need not take a predetermined form. Say our story is about a murder, and we are uncertain as to what method the assailant should use to commit the crime. We may breakthrough to the realization that the victim should fall to his death while skydiving. Then again, we may breakthrough to the realization that the victim should be electrocuted in a hot tub, injected with a lethal drug, or tossed off the roof of a high building. Each is a possible direction.

Up to the point where our depiction of evolution now stands, each threshold could lift the universe in only one evolutionary direction. The universe was in such a simple state that only one evolutionary direction existed. In the period of structural advancement we are about to explore, such is no longer the case. In our expanded model of the creative process, the threshold not only represents a leap to a more advanced evolutionary level but a crossroads or a turning point. As if it were the breakthrough experienced by the writer, it is a pivotal moment, the instant at which the universe has the potential to set forth in one of a number of alternative evolutionary directions.

What, then, determines these alternative directions, and what determines the specific one evolution will follow? To answer these questions, we must incorporate certain related concepts into our model of the creative process. I lump these concepts together as the ability of the creative process to *build on and creatively discard the old to create the new*. Like before, the easiest way to introduce these ideas is to look at how they reveal themselves on the human level. So, we return to our example of the writer.

While composing our murder story, the choices the author makes early in the writing process determine the choices available later in the writing process. If the author decides to make the story's victim a ninety-five-year-old kindergarten teacher bedridden in a nursing home, it would not make sense to have him murdered while skydiving or while lounging in a hot tub. More reasonable alternatives would be the injection of a lethal dose of morphine or the withholding of a lifesaving treatment.

Likewise, the direction taken at this point in the story's writing determines the alternative directions available further along in the story's writing. Say the author decided to make the victim a motion picture stuntman and to have him die while jumping off a bridge. Future turning points could lead to a plot about the man's partner tracking down the killer and bringing him to justice. Then again, if the victim was our ninety-five-year-old kindergarten teacher, and he was killed by an overdose of morphine, the assailant could be the victim's wife. The story might then be about a mercy killing and a woman's struggle to overturn a euthanasia law.

We can think of evolution as delineated by a series of thresholds. Most denote minor shifts in evolutionary direction. A few denote major shifts. In either case, the alternative evolutionary directions available at each juncture are established by those that came before. The expansion of consciousness in the universe's first evolutionary stage made possible the doubling of entities of consciousness in the universe's second evolutionary stage, which made possible the formation of relationships in the universe's third evolutionary stage. New evolutionary levels are built on old evolutionary levels.

The above illustration explains why there are only certain alternative evolutionary directions available at each threshold, but what determines the actual direction taken?

Here our answer is more intriguing, for we must explore a dimension of the creative process that is less defined than any we have encountered—a characteristic of consciousness and the way it behaves. Once again, we will introduce this aspect of the creative process on the human level.

While drafting our murder story, the author may take off in one direction only to at a later point realize he had made a mistake. Say the writer decided to make his victim our ninety-five-year-old kindergarten teacher. As we have seen, this could lead to a story about euthanasia. Perhaps, though, the author had setout to write a thriller packed with gunfights and car chases. The euthanasia plot might lead to a story with greater social significance, but it would not fulfill the author's need.

The author's choice to make his victim an elderly man felt right at the time, otherwise he would not have made it, but it led his writing in a wrong direction. As any author will tell you, the writing process is plagued by wrong directions. In each case, the writer must go back and try another approach.

In earlier chapters, we depicted the creative process as mechanistic, even mathematical. Indeed, it demonstrates these qualities. Yet, within the bounds established on the mechanical level, the process is free and dynamic. Within the range set by the number of alternative evolutionary directions, there is no precise mechanism to determine what evolutionary course to follow. The process is distinguished by a pattern of groping and trial and error. To behave as such is the nature of consciousness. The more evolved the consciousness the greater its freedom of action.

This brings us to our final point. If at each threshold, the creative process has the ability to branch in one of a number of alternative evolutionary directions and the direction taken need not be right, what happens to the incorrect evolutionary lines that result? What happens to everything created that turns out to have no enduring value in the end-game of evolution?

When our author completes the final draft of his murder story, it may be ten pages long. But to arrive at this number of pages, he may have written twenty, thirty, forty, or fifty pages. Writing is as much a process of rewriting as of initial composition. Yet, removing an obsolete storyline is not merely a matter of pressing the computer's delete key.

When rewriting, the author may keep a sentence or a paragraph here and there, move others, and delete still others. He may head in one direction, abandon that course, and return later to retrieve certain elements. Deleting text is not an easy matter because the parts that need to go may have been hard to create and tend to have a life of their own. But what is not needed must fall away. When reworking his text, the author reduces the number of alternative directions available at each juncture until the story reaches its final form. The author reshapes what he has written, building on and discarding the old in support of his overall creative effort. Rewriting is a creative activity.

When we consider the above point, our model of the creative process acquires a second dimension. On one hand, we see the creative process drive evolution forward. On the other hand, we see it reshape earlier evolution in support of the leading edge of evolutionary advance. The creative process brings into existence the new, while at the same time it reshapes the old, expanding on certain elements and discarding others.

In general, then, the creative cycle and threshold continue to form the basis of our model. But above this level, the creative process loses its rigidity. Emptiness remains the driving force. Uncertainty remains the obstacle, and a more evolved experience of fulfillment remains the aim. But each threshold lifts consciousness, and therefore the experience of these factors, in a new direction and to a more evolved and intensely felt level. As *Figure 7* shows, this intensification of consciousness gives rise to a characteristic pattern of evolutionary development. Like a two-edged sword, the creative process builds on the old to thrust evolution to successively higher stages. As it does, earlier stages reshape in support or—the obsolete remnants of once leading-edge evolution—fall from existence.

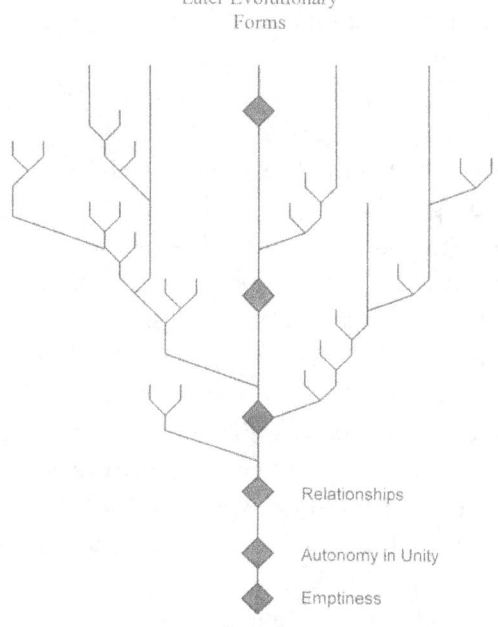

Later Evolutionary
Forms

Relationships

Autonomy in Unity

Emptiness

Earlier Evolutionary Forms

Fig. 7. Creativity's Pattern. With each threshold, the creative process builds on and creatively discards the old to create the evolutionary forms on which the future will rest. This gives rise to a characteristic pattern of evolutionary development. The straight line in the diagram's center emphasizes the point that, although evolution will branch in its trial and error, in the end there will be a clear ascent to greater consciousness.

Such summarizes our expanded view of the creative process and positions us to tie this view in with our evolution of consciousness account of cosmic formation.

Cycle after cycle, threshold after threshold, with all the characteristics we now associate with the creative process, relationships perceived one another and individual entities as the object of their need to create fulfillment and by doing so formed more intricate and consciousness relationships. These relationships perceived one another and earlier aspects of consciousness as object and by doing so formed still more complex and consciousness arrangements. With each threshold, the universe built on its previous level of organization to move forward—to grope to a higher level of organization. As the creative process thrust evolution to new levels, earlier levels reshaped in support or if no longer necessary vanished from existence.

This internal evolution manifested in the emergence of a series of familiar external forms.[1] Not long after what we call the universe's emergence, about 15 billion years ago, quarks came into existence, as did electrons and other indivisible particles. Soon after, protons and neutrons formed and came together to create the first atomic nuclei, the nucleus of the atom. About 300 thousand years later, nuclei captured electrons to form the first hydrogen, helium, and other simple atoms. These simple atoms came together about 700 thousand years after emergence to create the first hydrogen, helium, and other simple molecules.

At this point, the leading edge of evolution jumped to a celestial scale where not long after molecular development, the first clouds of stellar gas aggregated, composed largely of hydrogen and helium. About 1 billion years after emergence, the first celestial bodies formed—the objects that with their luminescence we would later call stars. About 2 billion years after emergence, the first proto-galaxies took shape. During the next 5 billion years, the first galaxies, galactic clusters, and higher levels of cosmic order came into existence.[2]

From here, evolution's leading edge returned to a microscopic scale, where about 8 billion years ago, the first heavy elements and ionic compounds came into existence, elements that are formed within stars. Finally,

1. The following paragraphs describe the sequence in which cosmologists theorize various external forms came into existence, a scenario that is reasonably supported by thought and observation.

2. In accordance with astronomical thought and observation, our evolution of consciousness view tells us that cosmic formation demonstrates organization at every level. At its earliest and most primitive level, this would reflect the structure of perception that existed when the universe crossed the threshold of autonomy in unity.

not long after this development, evolution's forward arrow returned to the macroscopic, and the first solar systems that contained planets made from heavy elements and ionic compounds organized.

As frequently cited as the above scenario of cosmic evolution may be, we must realize that it, like many scientific edifices, is a work subject to refinement. In particular, we must not place too much emphasis on dates. Dates serve mainly to help us keep our bearing in time. We should not take them as proven or absolute, especially when we consider the accelerating nature of time and evolution. Despite the fragility of the above account of cosmic emergence, its usefulness as a time-line is clear. It is, of course, only when we look beyond the framework of dates and events that we can grasp the transformation, or "cosmogenesis" as Teilhard called it, that it charts.

The external, we must remember, is not the "end-and-all" of creation, the universe's paramount state of being. The time-space fabric of the universe is a manifestation of the internal, a construct of consciousness in transformation. Between thresholds, we have advancement on a given evolutionary level. Across thresholds, we have a jump to a new evolutionary level.

When, for example, the creative process lifted the structure of perception we associate with the subatomic particle across the threshold to the structure of perception we associate with the atomic nucleus, the focus of evolution left subatomic formation. It engaged in proton and neutron arrangement and gave rise to nuclei. When the creative process lifted the structure of perception we associate with the nucleus across the threshold to the structure of perception we associate with the atom, the focus of evolution left nuclei formation. It engaged in the gathering of electrons about the nuclei and gave rise to the atom.

Here we see a familiar pattern. Old structural levels made possible new structural levels. The creative process built on previous evolutionary forms to create new evolutionary forms. Yet, the evolution of the cosmos did not take place in the tidy, stair-step manner our analysis may suggest, for we must not forget that the creative process also discarded the old.

Figure 8 will help us see this. As if it were a comet followed by its tail, we see evolution's forward line, or arrow, advance to greater complexity and consciousness and its trailing line, or arrow, advance to less complexity and consciousness.

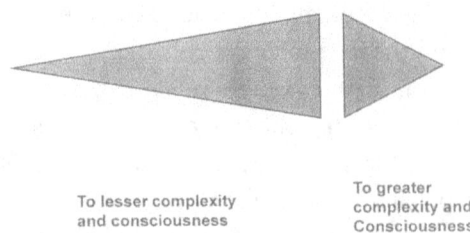

To lesser complexity
and consciousness

To greater
complexity and
Consciousness

Fig. 8. Evolution's Two Arrows. Locked forever in the present, the leading arrow of the universe's overall creative process advances evolution toward greater complexity and consciousness while the trailing arrow advances evolution toward less complexity and consciousness.

When, for example, the creative process thrust evolution's leading edge across the threshold from the level of the subatomic particle to the level of the nucleus and then to the level of the atom, not all subatomic particles were needed. The subatomic level realigned, and those particles not necessary to support atomic structure fell into obsolescence. Physicists have identified a great number of subatomic particles, but only the proton, neutron, electron, and a handful of others exist under any but the most "high-energy" and thus primitive evolutionary conditions.

Like the process of writing experienced by our author, as the creative process drove cosmic evolution forward, early levels reshaped in support or fell out of existence. This restructuring followed the same pattern of cycles and thresholds as forward evolution. As we have established, the process of building on and discarding the old is a creative activity. Looked at from another angle, creative activity on later evolutionary levels determined and thus regulated creative activity on earlier levels. Certain earlier levels flourished. Others dwindled and disappeared.

One may ask how many alternative evolutionary directions were tried and abandoned before nuclei and electrons combined to form the first atom or before atoms combined to form the first molecule. How many paths were charted and abandoned before the universe struck on the remarkable system of relationships that characterize subatomic, atomic, and simple molecular structure and that made possible the future in which we exist? During the earliest phases of cosmic evolution, there were not many alternative directions available at each juncture. The universe was yet in a simple state. But where no remnants exist, we may never know the actual branches of the universe's cosmic ascent.

Our understanding of the creative process, however, does shed light on two aspects of cosmic evolution whose essential nature is illusive, if not entirely baffling, when examined from a purely external point of view. They are *matter* and *movement*.

To begin with, recall that from the standpoint of the universe as a whole each overall creative cycle manifested in one overall click of time and in one overall rebirth of space. Also, recall that each relationship generated its own local creative cycles. It created its own region of relative time and space.

As internal aspects of greater consciousness emerged, and the structure of perception they embodied became more complex, the number of local creative cycles with respect to each overall creative cycle increased. When the nucleus evolved to become a part of the atom, which evolved to become a part of the molecule, local time-space became more relative. Each subsequent level became more defined, more stable in time-space. External manifestation became more solid. Each level more distinctly embodied the characteristics we associate with matter.

Similarly, as local external manifestation became increasingly cohesive, the growing differentiation between local and overall cyclic behavior created what from the human vantage was the effect of physical movement. As relationships changed, the universe's cyclic rebirth of time-space and the successive manifestations it generated with respect to local creative activity produced the characteristic of physical objects in motion through space. Likewise, due to the rate of the universe's overall cyclic rebirth, we would expect a maximum obtainable velocity of an object in the universe's external manifestation. The speed of light?

Overall, as the creative process brought forms of greater autonomy and consciousness into existence, external manifestation became more familiar. On a microscopic scale, structure of perception manifested in such established characteristics of physical behavior as bonding, attraction, and repulsion. The four forces of physics—gravity, electromagnetism, and the strong and weak forces, active in the atomic nucleus—solidified, united in that they are a way to account for the behavior of the internal on various levels of the relationship. Gravity, for example, is not the force the draws planets to a sun to form a solar system; it is how we externally characterize the structure of perception that constitutes a solar system. On a macroscopic scale, stars, planets, and other celestial bodies displayed intricate patterns of movement and association. A heavens closer to the one we know and observe took shape.

In the cosmos, there are many forms of structure. We find subatomic particles, atoms, molecules, and ionic compounds. We find stars, planets, solar systems, galaxies, galactic clusters, and walls of galactic clusters. We find quasars, pulsars, black holes,[3] and white dwarfs. When we take into account the complexity of the cosmos and the variety of its structures, we come to a realization. What mechanism other than the creative process could underlie its evolution? What mechanism other than the creative process—the same process we experience within ourselves—has the capacity to unite mathematical certitude with creative freedom in a way that accounts for the universe's order and diversity? If we could transport ourselves back in time and witness the evolution of the cosmos, if we could lift the veil from our eyes and view the internal alongside the external, would we not be looking into the expanding consciousness that was the universe? Would we not be looking into the emerging mind that was creation? Was not the structure of the cosmos the mental expression of evolution?

By creative process, new evolutionary paths emerged, and old ones realigned or fell from existence. With each creative cycle, uncertainty, consciousness, and the universe's experience of fulfillment and the need for fulfillment increased. With each threshold, uncertainty collapsed, and the universe rose to a higher level of structural complexity. In this unity between internal and external, we discern the basis for Teilhard's law of "consciousness and complexity." This law states that as internal consciousness increases external manifestation becomes more complex.[4] In the evolution of consciousness view, the law of consciousness and complexity characterizes the formation of the cosmos. Cosmogenesis, however, was not without its end. Time accelerated, and space became more complex. Then the universe reached the point where it exhausted its potential to create fulfillment through cosmic formation. The universe faced a major

---

3. The creative process advances through cycles and thresholds, trial and error, and creative building on and discarding of the old. This tells us that a mechanism or mechanisms must exit on the cosmic level to eliminate what is no longer necessary to support the forward thrust of the universe's evolution.

4. Expressed in different ways, Teilhard's law of consciousness and complexity is central to his thought.

threshold in the course of its development. Uncertainty overwhelmed and collapsed. Consciousness turned in on itself and embraced itself as what it had become. All that we today take to be the cosmos fell into the realm of evolution's trailing arrow. As the physicist characterizes this point in evolution, the universe reached the stage where dark energy became dominant over dark matter. [5] The creative process gave rise to a new era of structural formation—to the level of the complex molecule.

5. For a brief discussion on dark matter and dark energy, see Chapter 7, note 3.

7

Design Over Structure

A T THE MOMENT THE cosmos reached the height of its evolutionary rise, at the instant the universe exhausted all potential to advance to greater consciousness and fulfillment through cosmic formation, the creative process locked on a fundamentally different evolutionary line. This line began with the organization of the first complex molecular arrangements. The universe engaged in the development of the *organic molecule*.

We will trace this line of evolutionary advance to its logical end in a moment. First, we need to address another issue. As evolution's leading shoot locked in the organic molecule, all that came before—all of cosmic evolution—fell in its wake. The cosmos and all it encompassed became part of evolution's trailing arrow. As it did, our depiction of evolution, like a ship returned from a voyage across an uncharted sea, makes land at a familiar port, for physical science is the study of the external manifestation associated with this cosmic restructuring. We have reached the point in our depiction of the universe's emergence and formation where we can reconcile our evolution of consciousness account to the views put forth by present-day science.

To address every aspect of scientific theory would of course exceed the book's reach. My objective is not to tie-in our evolution of consciousness account with that of science in detail but to lay the groundwork for such a unification of perspectives. It is my hope that people in the sciences will recognize the validity of this task and engage in its pursuit.

To begin with, recall that physical science encompasses a number of areas of theoretical thought. Among these are thermodynamics, quantum mechanics, classical mechanics, and general and special relativity. The goal of these theoretical edifices is to predict the behavior of matter within a certain range of its existence. And the validity of their respective models rests to a large degree on their ability to yield similar results in those areas where their range of applicability overlaps. Take special relativity, applicable to objects moving at a range of speeds including those near the speed of light, and classical, or Newtonian, mechanics, applicable to objects moving at velocities we are more likely to encounter in day-to-day life. The ability of the relativistic expression to, say, give about the same value for the kinetic energy of a truck traveling down a freeway or of the moon in its orbit around the Earth as the classical expression, lends evidence to validate both models, the further reaching relativistic approach in particular. The question then becomes over what range does our evolution of consciousness view overlap with; or, in a more general sense, how does it tie in with, the theoretical frameworks of science?

We can get a feel for this connection by way of an example from physical chemistry, a field that to one degree or another draws on all of physical science's major areas of theoretical pursuit. Let us look at the expression that describes the reaction between hydrogen and oxygen to form water:

$$2H_2(g) + O_2(g) \rightarrow 2H_2O(g) \qquad \Delta H = -8.03 \times 10^{-19} \text{ J}$$

The above chemical equation states that two hydrogen molecules, H, combine with one oxygen molecule, O, to form two water molecules, H_2O, releasing 8.03×10^{-19} Joules, J, of energy, ΔH. The "g" in parentheses indicates that these molecules are in the gaseous as opposed to the solid or liquid state.

Now, from an evolution of consciousness standpoint, if we let the arrow denote the middle of the equation, we have three simple molecules on the left and two complex molecules on the right. The reaction thus proceeded from a state of lower complexity to a state of higher complexity. External complexity reflects internal complexity, which reflects consciousness. By creative process, the three aspects of lower consciousness and less complex structure of perception on the left side of the formula crossed a threshold to break apart. Their component atoms then followed a different evolutionary path. They recombined into two aspects of greater consciousness and more complex structure of perception. In the process, the entities of consciousness that comprised the initial relationships moved from a less fulfilled state to a more fulfilled state. Correspondingly, their manifested structures moved from a high mass-energy state to a low mass-energy state, with the difference measured as a release of energy.

Another example will help us see this pattern of internal and external transformation. This time we will look at a nuclear reaction, the decay of uranium-236 to form rubidium and cesium:

$$\ce{^{236}_{92}U} \rightarrow \ce{^{90}_{37}Rb} + \ce{^{143}_{55}Cs} + 3\ce{^{1}_{0}n} \qquad\qquad Q = 166 \text{ MeV}$$

The above expression states that one uranium-236 atom, U, decayed to form one Rubidium-90 atom, Rb, one cesium-143 atom, Cs, and three neutrons, n, releasing 166 millielectron volts, MeV, of energy, here indicated by "Q." The energy released in a nuclear reaction is normally expressed in MeV; 1.0 MeV equals 1.60 x 10^{-13} Joules. The other figures indicate the element's atomic number.

In this example, we have one complex atom on the left side of the equation and two less complex atoms and three neutrons on the right side. As such, the reaction proceeded in the opposite direction as our previous example—from a state of greater complexity to a state of lesser complexity. By creative process, the more complex and conscious evolutionary level represented on the left crossed a threshold to become the less complex and conscious evolutionary level represented on the right. As with the chemical reaction of hydrogen and oxygen to form water, the entities of consciousness that comprised the initial relationships moved from a less fulfilled state to a more fulfilled state—with the reduction of "need" measured as a release of energy. Mass is a property of energy, which is a property of need.

A chemical or nuclear formula such as H_2O or $^{236}_{92}U$ is a way to map the structure of perception associated with a given aspect of consciousness. A chemical or nuclear expression is a way to describe the transformation of one level of consciousness and structure of perception across a threshold to another level of consciousness and structure of perception.

To further reconcile our view with that of science, let us jump to modern physics and the theory of general relativity. Einstein's general relativity reduces to a set of interlinked differential equations, commonly referred to as Einstein's field equations, a view of the universe where matter and gravity are dealt with in terms of time-space. Gravity, for example, is not seen as a force that attracts one object to another but, due to an object's mass, as a curvature of the time-space fabric in a way that relates the objects.

In effect, every object—from the quark to the galactic cluster to the cosmos in its entirety—exists within a region of time-space relative to its own being. Illustrative of this idea is the concept of multiple dimensions.[1] Imagine you are Captain Kirk aboard the starship Enterprise and you have orders to travel to a planet in a solar system in a distant galaxy. In everyday life, we impose four dimensions on our world: width, length, height, and time. These dimensions do not exist. They are an abstraction we created to make it easier to move from one location to another and to get there when we want. When traveling great distances through space, however, four dimensions are not enough. Captain Kirk would have to give his helmsman a set of coordinates for the time-space region in which his destination galaxy is located, say the galactic cluster. He would then have to give a set of coordinates for the galaxy and a set for the solar system. Coordinates within coordinates, four-dimensional boxes within four-dimensional boxes. We encounter relative time and space every day, but its effect is so small we are not aware of it. Indeed, our bodies incorporate multiple levels and a seemingly unfathomable number of time-space regions.

Every aspect of the external universe exists within, or more precisely, as a region relative to its own being. The theory of general relativity is a way to mathematically describe the gravitational aspect of what in this section of the book we have established a theoretical foundation to account for and take to be a fundamental aspect of the external on every level of its organization—relative time-space.

We have laid out a basic approach to integrating our evolution of consciousness ideas with traditional and modern physical science, but we need to give one area special attention. We must look at the theory many consider the foremost achievement of modern physical thought, science's big bang model of cosmic formation.

To begin with, sciences uses the term "big bang" to mean two things: First, it denotes the instant when it all began, the moment when time equaled zero. Second, it denotes the scenario through which the various forms of matter that make up the cosmos came into existence. According

---

1. The concept of multiple dimensions used by the physicist has nothing to do with the concept of multiple dimensions used by many in popular culture, which typically means alternative realities.

to the big bang model, the universe began as an infinitely dense and hot point that violently exploded. As time progressed, space expanded and cooled, and the four fundamental forces identified by physics that we talked about in the last chapter—weak, strong, gravity, and electromagnetism—came into existence. These forces caused the energy associated with the big bang to coalesce into more complex arrangements of matter and thus to give rise to the external forms we also previously discussed: quarks, nuclei, atoms, molecules, stars, and so forth.

Now, to connect this view to our own. If we were to take our evolution of consciousness account of cosmic formation and block out its internal aspects, if we were to ignore the cycles and thresholds and the trial and error of the creative process and plot only the external forms they produced and then went on to categorize the patterns of attraction and repulsion between these forms, what would cosmic emergence look like? I think much like a "big bang." At least we could interpret it in this way—as a complexification and outward expansion of the physical universe. My present opinion is that science's big bang model traces and explains in terms of physical interaction certain aspects of the external evolution we would expect to see from a universe whose nature is as an entity of expanding consciousness.

But like any external theoretical edifice, the big bang model has its weaknesses. This brings us to the overriding limitation of the big bang model of cosmic formation.

By definition, physics is the field devoted to the study of the universe's "physical" qualities. As the universe crossed the various thresholds that led to its evolution beyond subatomic, atomic, simple molecular and cosmic structure, the leading arrow of the universe's evolution left these levels. These levels fell into the universe's trailing arrow.

Activity on the universe's trailing arrow creates the predictable universe physicists so admire. As evolution advanced beyond cosmic formation, creative activity on the cosmic and earlier levels realigned in support. As a result, matter and energy behaved in consistent ways. This stability is revealed by the physical laws and by the constants in the physical laws. Time, as measured by radioactive decay, for example, takes place at a constant rate.

In a broader sense, the notion of the physical universe as on the trailing edge of the universe's evolution is illustrated by the second law of thermodynamics. This law states that in any spontaneous process, such as the chemical and nuclear reactions we cited, there is an increase in the entropy, or disorder, of the cosmos.[2] Matter may evolve to states of greater complexity: Stars may continue to form. Reactions may continue to produce substances with more complex structures. But the overall direction of evolution on its trailing edge is toward decline—toward the falling-away of what is not needed to support the universe's advance.

The overriding limitation of the big bang model of cosmic formation is that it uses physical theory—principles of symmetry, conservation, and probability derived by studying matter on evolution's trailing arrow—to explain cosmic formation—an event that took place on evolution's forward arrow. Consequently, the model's ability to account for the leading edge phenomenon of cosmic formation is limited. The creative process functions on evolution's leading and trailing edges. For this reason, the big bang model can map aspects of cosmic formation. But it lacks the reach to account for that formation in a fundamental way.

Take, for example, the concept of energy. In our evolution of consciousness view, the creative cycle generates energy, or the motivation to create fulfillment. In common reactions, or ones where a threshold is crossed, as much energy is created or expended in the forward reaction as in the reverse reaction and from an external vantage energy appears to be conserved. Limited in their view to the external, the makers of the big bang model therefore reasoned that since we cannot create or destroy energy the universe must have begun in a state of infinite heat and density. All the energy now, or that will ever be, in the universe must have been present in the beginning. This energy then differentiated into matter and the cosmos we observe.[3]

2. The second law of thermodynamics is expressed in a number of ways. The definition cited is common.

3. The theoretical existence of dark matter and dark energy suggests that the law of energy conservation may not be universally applicable in an expanding universe. Cosmologists have observed that galaxies rotate in a way that indicates a gravitational effect from an unseen source, dark matter, a form of matter that interacts exclusively or predominantly through the gravitational force and thus cannot be directly detected. Along with the existence of dark matter is dark energy, which they theorize pervades space at a constant level and thus increases as the universe expands, violating the conservation law. In the broader sense, could we not think of dark matter and dark energy as a way of externally describing an organizational force beyond the strong, weak, electromagnetic, and gravitational forces—the overriding organizational behavior of the cosmos as an evolution of consciousness? Astronomers postulate that the cosmos began to expand at an increasing rate about five billion years ago. Physicists characterize this point as the

The big bag model occupies a special place in cosmology and has advanced our understanding of cosmic formation in many ways. Yet, like a wide-screen movie trimmed to be seen on a square television set, the big bang model cuts away the internal aspects of cosmic formation to create a theoretical edifice that fits the portal of physics. When we ask cosmologists what gave rise to the infinitely dense and hot point they theorize as the universe's beginning, their answer is simple. The question falls outside the domain of physics.[4] We have the observed evidence of cosmic evolution: an expanding universe that in its past advanced from a state of lesser organization to a state of greater organization. If one assumes that the universe began in a state of infinite heat and density and that the weak, strong, electromagnetic, and gravitational forces are capable of organizing matter into successively more complex arrangements, the big bang model can account for cosmic evolution. If one questions these assumptions, the model cannot. Most cosmologists acknowledge that beyond the first few seconds of existence, it becomes a stretch to think that the fundamental forces of physics could account for the diversity and coherent complexification that defines cosmic evolution.

Science can predict the trailing edge behavior of matter with great accuracy, but it cannot say what matter is or why it came into being. Science can tell us the way things are but not necessarily why they are that way. Science has yet to decipher the meaning that underlies existence. In such, I believe, lies the greatest value of the evolution of consciousness view. When taken in its entirety, it can offer this level of explanation. Newtonian mechanics may not describe the world as relativity and quantum mechanics tells us it exists, but we can use classical equations to land a rover on mars. Relativity and quantum mechanics may not describe the

---

time dark matter, dominant during cosmic formation, became less important than dark energy, dominant during cosmic expansion. Is this not a way of externally characterizing the universe's crossing of the evolutionary threshold where cosmic formation fell into evolution's trailing arrow?

4. The unwillingness of cosmology to deal with the universe's initial point has led to a great deal of conjecture. Some cosmologists theorize that the universe began as a *quantum fluctuation*—or a change, or wrinkle, on the quantum level. Others theorize that the universe began when the necessary conditions randomly came into place. Statistically, such conditions could have occurred an infinite number of times and thus given rise to an infinite number of universes. Neither model tells us a great deal about the universe's origin. Rather, they demonstrate the length to which science will go to force reality to conform to a purely external point of view.

world as evolution of consciousness theory tells us it exists, but we can use contemporary physical theory to design a microcircuit or a nuclear power plant. The evolution of consciousness view does not supplant established scientific models; it enwraps them in a larger theoretical construct and as such offers a fundamentally new level of explanation.

If, as did Teilhard, we accept science's highest aim to be the creation of a coherent explanation of the universe as a whole—and I think there are those in the sciences who will settle for nothing less—science faces a juncture. Science confronts the most profound shift in thought in the three hundred years of its modern existence—the embracing of the internal point of view alongside the external. Is consciousness the fundamental substance of the universe? Is the creative process the unifying principle of nature that physics has for more than a century sought? Can we push back the boundaries of science to in a logical and supportable way look beyond?

As the book progresses, we will explore the relationship between science and the evolution of consciousness view on a variety of levels. At this point, it is time to set the matter aside and return to our internal depiction of the universe's evolution.

At the end of the universe's period of cosmic formation, aspects of consciousness perceived one another as the object of their need and, by doing so, evolved beyond crystalline structure and the collective aggregations associated with the ionic compound to create a new level of molecular organization. Externally, methane and ammonia combined with water, nitrogen, and hydrogen to create simple sugars, carbohydrates, and amino acids. The creative process gave rise to the first complex carbon-hydrogen based molecules—to the intricate chains and links scientists call organic. Yet, like at previous evolutionary levels, the organic molecule was a step along the way, the platform on which would rise more complex, conscious, and autonomous structural forms.

Definitive of this evolution was the *metabolic system*. During the late 1950s, scientists discovered that certain organic and even certain inorganic molecules—which suggests an evolutionary path abandoned and resurrected—could interact to create what were popularly called *dissipative structures*.[5] These chemical systems maintain and enhance structural complexity by importing matter from and exporting matter to

5. The most frequently cited example of a dissipative structure is the Belousov-Zhabotinsky reaction, discovered in 1958 and named for its Russian investigators.

their surroundings. By harnessing the energy locked in the structure of matter, the dissipative system regulates the tendency of its more primitive evolutionary components to decline to less complex states. Entropy builds within the system, but the system dissipates this entropy into its surroundings. The ability of such systems to maintain structural integrity against evolution's trailing arrow—or to regulate internal creative activity in support of the system's overall creative existence—we call *metabolism.*

Looked at in another way, in a metabolic system the atomic and molecular components that make up the system can be exchanged for other components. One hydrogen atom can be replaced with another hydrogen atom. One sugar molecule can be broken apart and another synthesized. The atoms that constitute a carbon chain may be different today than tomorrow—but the chain remains. With metabolism, the universe moved beyond the simple organization of parts to form more complex structural arrangements. Structure superseded components to become the focus of the universe's evolutionary advance.

When we shift our view to the internal, an even more fundamental characteristic of the metabolic system reveals itself. Up to this point in our depiction of evolution, the various internal aspects of consciousness we have encountered perceived one another as the object of their need and, by doing so, created relationships and thus more complex and conscious aspects. What marked the threshold to metabolism was a new type of aspect perception. Like earlier aspects of consciousness, one metabolic system can perceive another as the object of its need, but the system sustains its existence by the perception of itself as the object of its need. Like a minuscule expression of the universe, the metabolic system embodies the consciousness to grow and evolve—the awareness to fully sustain its own creative process.

Moreover, the metabolic system exists through interaction with its surroundings. This introduces us to the concept of *environment* and directs our discussion to a familiar location. Central to the evolution of the metabolic system and its environment was the Earth.

Current theory suggests that the Earth formed 4.6 billion years ago from a cloud of stellar gas and heavy element debris that drew in on itself to create the sun and planets. But the Earth at the time of its formation was nothing like the Earth we know today. At its beginning, our planet existed as a super-heated ball of molten iron, silicone, aluminum, and other elements. By about 4.4 billion years ago, it had cooled to the point where the crust had solidified, and an atmosphere of methane, ammonia, nitrogen, hydrogen, water vapor, and carbon dioxide, with little gaseous oxygen, had accumulated. Then, by about 4.1 billion years ago, water vapor in the atmosphere had condensed to form oceans.

The evolution of the Earth and its oceans, however, was not what caused the development of the metabolic system. In the evolution of consciousness view, the universe has only one forward arrow of advance. The emergence of the metabolic system and the emergence of the environment to sustain its existence are two dimensions of one development. The environment did not give rise to metabolism, and metabolism did not give rise to its environment. Both were created by and advanced through the cycles and thresholds of the universe's creative process. Both evolved as an expression of a single evolutionary movement. The evolution of the Earth was not a disassociated event, insignificant in the vastness of the cosmos. It was an integral part of this movement.

With this thought, we have reached the point where we can complete what at the beginning of the chapter we had set out to do, and that is to trace to its most significant turning point the evolutionary line begun by the emergence of the organic molecule.

The development of the first metabolic system was followed by the development of more complex metabolic systems. This evolution took place in two ways. Metabolic systems advanced through the cycles and thresholds of their own, local creative process and through the perception of one another as object to create relationships, or integrated systems of metabolic reactions. In both cases, the autonomy and consciousness associated with the metabolic system increased, and structure of perception became more complex and disassociated from components. Metabolic development accompanied environmental development. The Earth's early oceans were surely a soup of organic molecules and metabolic activity. Then, about four billion years ago, the universe exhausted its potential to create fulfillment through the evolution of the metabolic system and its associated surroundings.

The creative process builds on the old to bring forth the new. The refinement of the metabolic system made possible a major evolutionary development—the leap that would propel the universe beyond its age of structural formation and into its next major evolutionary era, the period of advancement defined by the existence and evolution of *Life*.

Fifteen billion years ago, the universe emerged from a state of emptiness. From an internal point of view, the universe's evolution unfolded as an expansion of consciousness followed by the doubling of the fundamental entity of consciousness that resulted and by the perception between entities to create relationships. These relationships perceived one another as object to create successively more complex and consciousness arrangements until the universe reached the point where, with the advent of metabolism, it embraced structure as separate from and above components and the creative process as fully functioning on the level of the relationship. From an external point of view, the universe's evolution unfolded as an expansion of space and uniform energy followed by the doubling of the fundamental region of energy that resulted and by the arrangement of these regions, or particles, to form clusters. These clusters organized into increasingly complex structures, giving rise to a time-space fabric that included atoms, molecules, the cosmos, organic molecules, and metabolic systems.

The universe once again faced an evolutionary turning point. Uncertainty overwhelmed and collapsed. The universe turned in on itself and grasped itself as what it had become. Externally, metabolic systems perceived one another as object to create an altogether new class of metabolic systems. The first single-celled life-forms emerged, entities capable of *reproduction.* Like the engineer who designs a car built on a distant assembly line, the universe rose above the level of structural formation and set forth in its next logical direction. By way of cellular reproduction, the creative process relegated structure and its formation to the local level—to the level of the cell. The universe not only embraced structure as separate from and above components but also marked the turning point that I believe constitutes the emergence of life.[6] The universe crossed the threshold to embrace *design as separate from and above structure.*

---

6. Many people choose not to draw the line between life and pre-life as sharply as I do. Teilhard, for example, saw "Life" as present at the simplest levels of organization. In my view, the threshold of design over structure marks a clear boundary between the consciousness associated with life and the consciousness associated with pre-life.

PART THREE

Life

8

The Cell

IN OUR ACCOUNT OF evolution, the universe advanced from the time of the first single-celled entity, which appeared about four billion years ago, to a point about one hundred thousand years ago through the design of life, or as Teilhard termed it, "orthogenesis." In this and the next two chapters, we look at the complexification of organic form that resulted from the refinement of life's design and relate it to an underlying evolution of consciousness. Along the way, we address such issues as sex, death, sleep and dream, thought and learning, the will to survive, and the willingness for self-sacrifice. The third part of the book concludes as our depiction reaches the point where the universe marks its next great evolutionary milestone and ascends the developmental plateau that allows it to advance into its fourth major evolutionary period, that of understanding. I call this threshold *reflection*.

At the onset of the evolutionary period of life, the universe existed as an entity of consciousness that embodied a complex internal and external structure. This structure included subatomic, atomic, molecular, cosmic, complex molecular, metabolic, and cellular levels. The trailing edge of the creative process was locked in reshaping all but the most recent of these evolutionary levels. The leading edge was locked in the advancement of the single-celled life-form. In this chapter, we look at the cell and the evolutionary development it embodied.

Before doing so, I must address a related issue. It is with some reluctance that I bring up the matter because of the strong feelings any conclusion I reach will evoke. But our account of the universe would not be complete without a brief discussion in its regard. The issue is the evolution of life beyond the Earth.

As it now stands, science offers no all-encompassing explanation for the emergence of life. The reason is that we find such an explanation on the internal level—the threshold of design over structure—and science has chosen not to explore this level. Science can describe in detail the organic molecule, the metabolic system, and the cell, but it provides no general model to account for the evolution that took place between these forms. But science, as science must, has to say something about the matter. So, it offers the explanation it provides whenever it has no explanation, and that is to say that the beginning of life was a *random* event.

Specifically, science tells us that life on Earth began when the necessary environmental conditions existed and that these conditions were the result of chance factors: the development of the Earth's early methane, ammonia, and carbon dioxide atmosphere, the amount of energy available from the sun and geothermal sources. It therefore follows that in a cosmos composed of billions of stars orbited by billions of planets that these conditions could have occurred in a statistically significant number of locations. If we assume that life is the product of randomly occurring environmental conditions, we can conclude that it exists throughout the cosmos.

But when we embrace the evolution of consciousness view, the notion of life as the product of randomly occurring environmental conditions has no meaning. From our perspective, life is not a haphazard statistical event and neither is its environment. The notions of randomness and probability have no meaning beyond their use as a tool to impose an external view on an internal universe.[1] To us, life and environment are the result of a coherent evolution of consciousness—a logical, unavoidable, unfolding of awareness in the course of the universe's advance. As scientists have long marveled, if the least thing were different about the universe—the boiling point of a substance off by a fraction of a degree, a constant in a physical law off by the hundredth decimal point, water increasing in density when it froze rather than crystallizing and decreasing in density—life could not exist. In the evolution of consciousness view, such coherence in nature is not a haphazard development or the work of an all-knowing, all-powerful, never-changing creator—not to deny

1. To illustrate the practical aspect of the idea of randomness, think of a gas in a container. The individual gas molecules are in motion, constantly colliding with one another and with the walls of the container. From the standpoint of the individual molecule, collisions are not random; they are the consequence of speed and trajectory. To model the behavior of a gas in terms of individual collisions, however, would be prohibitively complex. Better to think of the collisions as random and characterize the behavior of the gas in terms of pressure and temperature.

the existence of a god—but what we would expect. Earlier evolutionary levels align in support of later evolutionary levels. The cosmos is not the medium in which evolution takes place, but an expression of prior evolution, a trailing-edge manifestation of the consciousness—of the mental construct—we call the universe and that exists in support of creation's continued advance.

Given this view and our notion of trial and error, what can we conclude about the evolution of life in the cosmos? Reasonably, the precursors of life, organic molecules and simple metabolic systems, emerged throughout the physical universe or were widespread. Even simple cellular and multicellular life-forms could have widely evolved. But at some point, probably early on, the universe focused in on life and its design. As Teilhard concluded, the widespread advance of life throughout the physical universe would serve no purpose.[2] The universe's evolution has only one leading edge of advance. If we embrace the idea of the universe as an evolution of consciousness, life rose to its apex in, and along with, only one location, one corner of the structure of perception we call the cosmos. That spot was the Earth.

I realize that many readers will find this conclusion disconcerting. But as we progress and the evolution of consciousness view unfolds in its entirety, I think the uniqueness and importance of life on Earth will become self-evident. I find the possibility empowering. If we are alone in the cosmos, each action we take not only affects our life and the lives of those around us, but conceivably humanity and, if we consider humanity to be life's highest expression, the universe.

Now, we return to the early Earth and immerse ourselves in the waters of its first oceans. There we find a rich assortment of organic molecules, metabolic systems, and the earliest cells.

The first cells were probably simple bacteria and cyanobacteria, the latter traditionally called blue-green algae, or less complex precursors of such entities. As commonly classified, these life-forms would fall into, or be most closely related to, the category of single-celled entities called *Prokaryotae*.

Like all cells, prokaryotic cells are enclosed by a cell membrane and contain genetic material called deoxyribonucleic acid, or DNA. But unlike in more advanced cells, the DNA in the prokaryotic cell is a single

---

2. The importance of life on Earth, and in particular of humanity, is a central concept in Teilhard's writings.

molecule in direct contact with the cell's fluid and not contained in a cell nucleus.

The small amount of oxygen present in the early atmosphere suggests that the first cells maintained an anaerobic, or non-oxygen based, metabolism. Such entities most likely derived energy by transforming hydrogen and carbon dioxide into methane. The presumed descendants of these methane-producing entities are found in oxygen-free environments in sewers, in cow stomachs, in thermal vents at the bottom of the ocean, and in places such as the hot springs of Yellowstone National Park in North America.

It is also reasonable that at an early date cells developed a metabolism based on photosynthesis, or the ability to convert solar energy into chemical energy. The absence of atmospheric oxygen would have prevented the buildup of a protective ozone layer, so photosynthesis would have used ultraviolet light to breakdown methane and release hydrogen. It is also conceivable that at an early date cells were linked by a hydrogen-methane cycle similar to the oxygen-carbon dioxide cycle that exists between plants and animals today.

Regardless of the specific function metabolism may fulfill, from a morphological standpoint it serves one purpose—to export entropy, or disorder, into the environment and, by doing so, to maintain or enhance structure. In metabolism, certain compounds pass through the cell's outer membrane and take part in chemical reactions. These reactions synthesize some substances to build or repair cell structure and breakdown others to produce energy or to facilitate the removal of waste products. At every level of activity, the cell displays a relationship between structure and function.

The above discussion provides us with a look at the early cell from an external point of view. As we might expect, when we refocus our eyes and include the internal, the cell's structure and function take on a somewhat different character.

Internally, we see the cell as a conscious entity made-up of aspects of lesser consciousness related through a complex structure of perception. The cell's overall consciousness enwraps the level of consciousness associated with the metabolic system, which enwraps the level of consciousness associated with the molecule, and so on down the evolutionary ladder to the smallest subatomic particle. From an internal standpoint, the cell is made-up of aspects of consciousness nestled within aspects of consciousness.

But structure of perception is not a static state of being. The cell's overall structure is sustained by the cycles and thresholds of the cell's overall creative process. This creative process enwraps the level of creative activity associated with the cell's metabolic systems. The creative activity associated with the cell's metabolic systems enwraps the creative activity that sustains molecular structure of perception, which enwraps the creative activity that sustains atomic and lower levels of structure of perception. Like a web of perception folded in on itself, the cell is made-up of systems of creative activity nestled within systems of creative activity.

How, then, does the cell regulate this creative activity? A metabolic system has the ability to speed up or slow down or to jump to a new level of function. It has the potential to evolve through the cycles and thresholds of its creative process. What makes this internal evolution possible when it benefits the cell and prevents it from taking place when it threatens the cell? Externally, such control manifests through the action of enzymes and other means of chemical mediation. Internally, intracellular regulation, like all aspects of cell function, is a creative process. In a manner analogous to the way older evolutionary structures reshape in support of creative activity on evolution's leading edge, more deeply embedded levels of cell creative activity function in support of less deeply embedded levels. Intracellular regulation is based on control by creative process—or the alignment of creative activity within the cell in support of the cell's overall creative existence.

The creative power contained within the prokaryotic cell is particularly apparent when it comes to the act of reproduction, termed *binary fission*, or simple cell division.

When the universe crossed the threshold of design over structure, it relegated the task of structural formation to the level of the cell. To accomplish this task, the cell had to maintain an awareness of its structure and of the procedure needed to reproduce that structure. The cell's awareness of its structure and reproductive procedure had an external manifestation. The threshold of design over structure marked the embodiment of a DNA molecule.

Externally, we can think of DNA as containing the coded information the cell needs to maintain and reproduce its structure. Simple, asexual, cell division, for example, results in two identical daughter cells, each containing a copy of the cell's original genetic code. During the cell's reproductive phase, the cell grows to roughly double its normal size. As this takes place, the cell's DNA duplicates through a process of chemical recognition and the breaking and forming of bonds. Once duplication is complete, one copy of the DNA molecule moves to either side of the cell. The cell constricts in the middle and separates to become two entities.

As we might expect, cell division appears different on the internal level. Internally, we see the act of reproduction as an expression of the consciousness manifest in the cell's DNA molecule. During the reproductive phase, the activity of the cell's overall creative process steps up. In support, creative activity on the level associated with the cell's metabolic systems increases. With each local and overall creative cycle, cell structure of perception duplicates. With each local and overall threshold, replication enters a new stage, to climax in cell division.

Whether viewed externally or internally, cell division is an expression of precisely controlled creative activity directed toward a predetermined end. Its role is significant, the elemental mechanism that brings organic structure into being.

In our brief discussion of the cell, we have only begun to explore its nature. Details aside, I hope we have achieved what I feel is most important and that is to open our eyes to the cell's internal dimension and to contrast this dimension with its external side. It is not that one point of view offers a better vantage than the other. Both reveal certain qualities of the cell. Rather, when we embrace the two together, the cell appears as so much more.

Yet, from the standpoint of the universe as a whole, the cell's beauty lies not in its structure and function but in its ability to act as the medium through which life's design advanced. By the cycles and thresholds and the trial and error of the creative process, the universe built on the level of awareness embodied in the first cells to create, reproduce, and socially organize new unicellular life in an expanding global biosystem.

This expansion of life took place through a sequence of evolutionary stages. To a reasonable extent, these evolutionary stages are documented by fossil remains and by evidence such as biogenous carbon deposits formed as the result of photosynthesis.

By about 3.5 billion years ago,[3] the first cells capable of conducting photosynthesis using a lower, less energetic wavelength of light than ultraviolet had emerged. This allowed cellular entities to create carbohydrates from carbon dioxide and water while giving off oxygen and led to a gradual buildup of oxygen in the atmosphere and to the formation of an ozone layer.

By about 3.2 billion years ago, the growing consciousness embodied within the single-celled entity had manifested in two new developments. Blue-green algae perceived one another as the object of their need, but too primitive to form more tightly bound relationships, arranged to create what we might call the first social structures, highly collective mat-like organizations of cells similar to those seen in pond slimes today. Perhaps as early, the first cells containing external appendages called cilia and flagella emerged. These whip-like extensions made it possible for the cell to propel itself through the water.

By about 1.4 billion years ago, atmospheric oxygen had reached the level needed to sustain aerobic, or oxygen based, metabolism. The use of oxygen increased the cell's ability to downgrade energy stored in the glucose molecule, and metabolism became more efficient. This made another development possible. Prokaryotic cells perceived one another as object to combine and form a new class of single-celled entities called *Eukaryote*. Eukaryotic cells are defined by a cell nucleus that contains most of the cell's DNA and by internal structures called *organelles* that, like the prokaryotic cells from which they originated, are enclosed by a membrane and contain their own DNA.

The complexity and consciousness associated with the eukaryotic cell was the foundation for two developments that, by about 1.2 billion years ago, would forever change the face of life. They were sexual reproduction and the internalization of death, or lifespan.

To understand the nature of these developments, we need to return to an idea we introduced several chapters ago, the notion of accelerating time as it relates to evolution. As we described, time accelerates when the number of local creative cycles that take place per overall creative cycle increases. Thus, as the universe advanced and its structure of percep-

---

3. This date and the dates associated with other events in the chapter represent the general range of times at which the respective developments are thought to have taken place. Other published dates may vary.

tion became more complex, time moved at a faster rate. The pace of the universe's evolution quickened.

In cell sexual reproduction, the DNA of two members of the cell species intermingles. This intermingling of genetic material increases the potential for structural variation to develop in the cell's offspring. As the pace of time increased, sex emerged as a mechanism to inject *novelty* into the creative process—as a means to amplify the number of alternative evolutionary directions available at each threshold. Sexuality reflected the accelerated rate of the universe's trial and error.

Whereas sex involved the leading arrow of evolution, lifespan involved the trailing arrow. Prior to the point where lifespan became ingrained in the consciousness of the cell's genetic makeup, entities met death only through natural hazard. In theory, the first cell to emerge in the universe could be in existence today. But as the pace of evolution quickened, so did the rate at which earlier creative forms became obsolete. Internalization of death was the mechanism through which an accelerated creative process could more rapidly discard the old.

Before the development of sex and lifespan, reproduction did not constitute a sequence of generations as we normally think of it. Whatever introduction of novelty that occurred probably took place by way of DNA molecules dissolved in the water or transferred on a carrier such as a virus. With sex and lifespan, ancestry began and successive generations formed a lineage.

Here we need to shift the focus of our discussion. We have looked at the internal and external nature of the cell and its evolution, but we cannot separate the cell from its environment.

From the standpoint of the individual cell, environment consists of its immediate surroundings, measured by the distance at which the cell can interact with metabolic components and with other cells in whatever social organization it may participate. As more complex and conscious cells emerged—evidenced by cilia and flagella and the ability of the cell to relocate itself—this distance increased. The cell became more aware of its environment.

From the standpoint of a species of cells, environment consists of the interaction that takes place between two or more species. A species of single-celled entities that consumes oxygen and releases carbon dioxide, for example, would interact with a species that consumes carbon dioxide and releases oxygen. This level of environment we will call the *ecosystem*.

From the standpoint of the ecosystem, environment consists of the interaction that takes place between two or more ecosystems. Ultimately, we define the extent of this environment by an ecosystem's place within the Earth's overall system of geological, biological, and climatological activity. This level of environment we will loosely refer to as the level of the *biosphere*.

Each of these environmental categories represents one or more levels of consciousness and creative function. One level would be associated with the cell and another with its social structure. Another level, or group of levels, would be associated with the ecosystem and with interacting ecosystems. The highest level at the point in evolution dominated by the cell would be associated with the biosphere. Like life, environment is made-up of systems of consciousness and creative activity nestled within systems of consciousness and creative activity to form a greater whole—the Earth.

We have looked at cell structure and function and at the arrangement of cells to form social structure. We have looked at cell evolution, at the relationship between species and ecosystems, and at the relationship between ecosystems and the all-embracing whole we call the biosphere. But we must not forget that this evolution was the embodiment of a greater evolution, of an overriding movement to create greater consciousness. The advance of life and Earth was the advance of the universe in its drive to achieve a more evolved state of fulfillment.

Threshold after threshold, more complex and conscious single-celled entities emerged. Cell function reached new levels of complexity, and cell awareness of environment extended to new distances. Social structure became less collective, progressing to the cell colony. By about 800 million years ago, *heterotrophy*, or the feeding by one species of life on another, had become widespread, and ecosystems and the biosphere reflected the complexity of this interaction. Then, by about 750 million years ago, the creative process had exhausted its potential to advance through the evolution of unicellular life. The universe crossed the threshold to a more complex form of biological structure and function. The first multicellular entities emerged.

9

Line of Consciousness

IN THE LAST CHAPTER, we left off with the development of the first multicellular entities. From an evolution of consciousness standpoint, the first multi-celled entities came into being when various single-celled entities perceived one another as the object of their need and, by doing so, combined to create a relationship. Over time, the creative process gave rise to more complex relationships that joined with other relationships to create entities with multiple levels of structure and function. Life-forms composed of organs and organ systems emerged. Along with the evolution of the organism, the Earth's biosphere evolved to reflect increasingly complex interaction between species and between ecosystems. Whether on the level of the organism or on the level of the environment, we define the refinement of life's design by a rise to greater consciousness. In this chapter, we follow this "line of consciousness" and explore the remarkable developments that took place during the course of its assent.

Our journey along life's line of consciousness begins during a period divided into two great geological eras. Paleontologists call the first of these eras the *Paleozoic*, which lasted from about 540 million years ago to about 245 million years ago. They call the second the *Mesozoic*, which began at the time the former ended and lasted to about 65 million years ago. The sequence in which new species evolved during these time spans is well documented by fossil evidence and scientific scrutiny.

At the beginning of the Paleozoic era, the surface of the Earth consisted of a vast ocean from which rose various landmasses. Most of these landmasses, or protocontinents as paleontologists call them, were situated in the tropics and southern hemisphere. Life was confined to the seas, which teamed with worms, sponges, mollusks, and other invertebrate organisms as well as with various types of algae and seaweed. The largest of these early life-forms was a cephalopod mollusk that had a shell about three meters, or ten feet, in length. The most noted was an arthropod called the trilobite that was particularly widespread.

By about 500 million years ago, the protocontinents that would one day form Europe and North America had come together to create a vast continental area, much of which was submerged beneath a shallow sea. In this and other aquatic regions, corals and clams flourished, as did primitive armored fish and other vertebrates. By about 450 million years ago, plants had colonized land, followed, 50 million years later, by animals. At the same time, rays, sharks, and other cartilaginous fishes roamed the oceans. By 370 million years ago, flying insects had emerged and forests of ferns and woody plants that grew to tree-like heights covered much of the land. Ultimately, these forests would decay to create many of the vast oil and coal reserves found in North America and other parts of the world.

By about 250 million years ago, the Earth's landmasses had come together to form a single supercontinent called *Pangaea*. Not long after, trilobites, many fishes, and a large number of other species died out in what some paleontologists consider the greatest mass extinction of all time. This extinction marked the spread and evolution of a more advanced class of life that rose out of the amphibian. The Paleozoic era had ended, ushering in the Mesozoic era, or the age of the reptile.

During the Mesozoic era, Pangaea split into two continents, the southern called *Gondwanaland*, the northern called *Laurasia*. Gondwanaland then split into what would become India, Africa, Australia, Antarctica, and South America, and Laurasia split into what would become Asia, Europe, and North America. Biologically, the Mesozoic saw the rise of many new life-forms, but none that has captured our attention more than the dinosaur.

The earliest dinosaurs were comparatively small creatures that rarely exceeded 4.5 meters, or 15 feet, in length. They ran on their hind feet and balanced their bodies against the weight of enormous tails. By 195 million years ago, the various species we hold dearest to our hearts had begun to emerge. These included the armor-plated stegosaurus, the rhino-like triceratops, the massive two-footed carnivore tyrannosaurus rex, and the heavy four-footed vegetarian apatosaurus. The marine reptile plesiosaurus had also evolved as had the species that to some is most endearing of all, pterodactylous, the great flying reptile with a wingspan of up to 11 meters, or 36 feet.

The dinosaur may define the Mesozoic era, but the age also saw the rise of many other species. These included birds and modern varieties of such common plants as oak, maple, holly, beech, poplar, laurel, walnut, magnolia, and sassafras. The period also saw the emergence of an animal class that represented the next step in the advance of life's design—the *mammal.*

Before we look at the evolution of the mammal, however, we need to tighten the scope of our analysis and look at the organism itself.

The earliest multicellular entities were little more than tightly bound clusters of cells. But, as the creative process advanced and more complex life-forms emerged, fundamental changes in anatomy and function came into being.

The most visible of these changes was a *circulatory system.* As life-form complexity increased, certain cells became isolated from contact with seawater. A system became necessary to transport nutrients into the organism and to carry waste products out of the organism. The first such circulator systems were little more than ducts through which seawater could flow. More advanced systems ranged from the vascular networks found in plants like kelp to the somewhat more sophisticated systems found in sea animals like jellyfish to the highly specialized digestive and cardiovascular systems found in fish, reptiles, and mammals.

In addition to a circulatory system, multicellular evolution embodied the development of a *nervous system.* In the nervous system, certain elements are devoted to reception of stimuli, others to processing stimuli, and still others to controlling any action invoked by such processing. This division of labor translates into a system made-up of a brain, sensory organs, and the network of nerves through which the brain connects with various parts of the organism's body. As more conscious organisms emerged, the organism's awareness of and ability to interact with its environment increased. This evolutionary trend manifested in the development of a more complex nervous system.

Multicellular evolution also saw the development of a *reproductive system.* In multicellular reproduction, the cell not only has the responsibility to duplicate its own structure but to do so in a way that contributes to the reproduction of the entire organism. The genetic information contained within the cell has to include a coded representation of overall organism structure and of the procedure necessary to reproduce that structure. The great variety of reproductive systems observed in plants and animals came about through the trial and error of the creative process as different means to execute this information.

When viewed as a whole, we see the multicellular life-form as an entity made-up of functional systems nestled within functional systems to create—at the apex of its expression—the network of organs and organ groups that defines the anatomy of higher life.

The above discussion gave us a feel for the physiology of the multicellular organism. Such is important, but our major interest lies beyond physical form. So, it is time to expand our discussion to include the organism's internal dimension.

In our view, the multi-celled life-form consists of a top level of consciousness and creative activity that enwraps successively lower levels of consciousness and creative activity. If the organism were a modern crocodile, its top level of consciousness and creative activity would be the level we associate with the organism itself—the level that recognizes the gazelle drinking at the edge of the pool. This level of consciousness and creative activity embraces the level we associate with the crocodile's various internal systems, which embraces the level we associate with its subsystems down to the level of the organ and the cell. The multi-celled life-form is made-up of systems of consciousness and creative activity nestled within systems of consciousness and creative activity.

This brings us to the question of regulation. Say our crocodile decides to take a bite out of the gazelle drinking at the edge of the pool. In response to this decision, the crocodile's nervous system signals various muscles throughout the animal's body to extend and contract in a specific manner. This activity requires oxygen, so the animal breathes faster and its heart beats more rapidly. Externally, such regulation manifests through enzymes, hormones, nervous system impulses, and other chemical and electrical means. Internally, the creative activity associated with the crocodile's heart and lungs supports the creative activity associated with its cardiovascular system, which supports the creative activity associated with its nervous system. As in the cell, system regulation is based on control by creative process—the alignment of creative activity within the organism in support of the organism's overall creative existence.

We generally think of the organism in terms of external function. The hormone epinephrine increases blood sugar. Life is the sum of information contained in DNA. At times, we may reduce these interactions to cause and effect relationships. Too much sunshine causes sunburn. Certain viruses and bacteria cause disease. In many respects, a purely external view—cause and effect or otherwise—is acceptable, and has proven effective in medicine and other pursuits. But when we open our eyes a bit wider and at least glimpse the organism's internal dimension, life appears as far more meaningful than the mere expression of genetic code.

We will see this clearly in a moment, for we need to address the one characteristic that more than any other defines consciousness on the level of the higher organism—the ability to think and to learn. Before we begin, I must make clear that the type of thought and learning we are about to discuss is not the same as the type of thought and learning we experience, that associated with the top level of human consciousness. In this chapter, we look at thought and learning on a simpler level, that associated with less complex life-forms—the level I call *abstract thought and learning*. I must also point out that the word "abstract" as used here refers to a type of thought and learning as opposed to, in its normal usage, a difficult concept.

In the evolution of consciousness framework, awareness, we must recall, is not the result of the structure and movement of matter. The structure and movement of matter reflect awareness. Abstract thought and learning are not the products of anatomical mechanics. They are not the outcome of brain wiring. They are the way the creative process behaves on the top level of organism consciousness. They are the manner of creative activity, the nature of consciousness, the way building on and creative discarding of the old takes place. This greatly simplifies our task to understand these facets of the organism. Our goal becomes to develop a model that will make it easier for us to visualize this manner of creative activity.

To begin with, recall that atomic and molecular aspects of consciousness perceive one another as the object of their need and, by doing so, create or breakdown a relationship. On the level of the cell, this permits certain substances in the cell's environment to pass through the cell's outer membrane and to participate in the bonding, attraction, and repulsion that on the atomic and molecular levels define metabolic activity. The cell's consciousness—the cell's awareness of the world around it—manifests through simple atomic and molecular recognition, the basis of which we find in our concept of perception of object. In what way, then, does the awareness of the more advanced organism reveal itself? How does our crocodile grasp the situation presented by the gazelle drinking at the edge of the pool?

The environment our crocodile perceives is more complex than that of the cell. In the crocodile's world, the animal must interact with other crocodiles and with the various creatures that share its pool or stop to drink, all of which to some degree look and behave differently. To deal with such complexity, the crocodile must simplify its world. It does this in a remarkable way. In part, the consciousness that is our crocodile is comprised of a mental, or *abstract*, representation of the animal's environment—manifest in nervous system structure of perception. In part, the consciousness of the higher organism consists of a model, of an internal construct, that utilizes atomic and molecular relationships to represent the world of the animal's experience.

To interact with its environment, then, our crocodile must relate the actual world to its abstract model of that world. This task begins with the animal's senses. When our crocodile first observed the gazelle at the edge of the pool, a stream of sensory impressions flooded into its body—sights, sounds, smells, the feel and taste of the water. By comparing this sensory representation of its world with the information contained in its abstract model of that world, the crocodile has the means to react as we expect a crocodile should. Its consciousness embraces its surroundings.

How, then, does this comparison between abstract and sensory representations take place, or more accurately how does the creative activity associated with this comparison take place? Here our explanation takes the turn that allows us to account for the dynamic patterns of thought and learning we find in the organism as opposed to the static comparison and feedback mechanisms we associate with a computer or a cybernetic system. The basis for our explanation lies in the creative process and in the pattern of cycles and thresholds that defines existence.

Motivated by the need to grasp the situation created by the gazelle, our crocodile's top level of consciousness folds in on itself: The animal perceives itself as the object of its need. As it does, the animal's sensory and abstract representations align through simple atomic and molecular recognition. With each creative cycle, the alignment of the sensory with the abstract establishes and refines patterns of nervous system structure of perception. With each threshold, uncertainty collapses to lift the animal beyond simple recognition to a higher level of awareness, to the fulfillment of its need—to a state of *comprehension*. Motivated by need, our crocodile creates the consciousness necessary to fulfill its need. Not only does our crocodile recognize the gazelle, it grasps the situation created by its presence—a potential meal.

Throughout an organism's life, sensory and abstract representations align, and the organism's internal model of its world develops. Abstract learning is a growth of consciousness, manifest in the refinement of an organism's internal model of the world. Abstract thought is the creative process that brings about that growth and refinement. By the cycles and thresholds and the trial and error of the creative process, the organism advances to greater awareness. It evolves within itself. It internalizes its world. It thinks and learns abstractly.

The internal view of thought and learning is a provocative aspect of the evolution of consciousness framework. Keep in mind while grappling with this view that, as we mentioned, the wiring of the brain does not give rise to consciousness. Rather, the wiring of the brain reflects consciousness. Creative activity builds nervous system structure of perception. Consciousness manifests in physical structure and not the other way around. The failure to recognize this relationship, I think, accounts for limitations in many contemporary theories on thought and learning and suggests bounds to the "intelligence" we can build into a simple comparison and reaction mechanism like a computer.

We will refine our view of thought and learning in the next couple of chapters. For the time being, it would be useful to look at certain ideas that emerge from this view. Like other aspects of the evolution of consciousness framework, it is a portal that allows us to understand many of life's most remarkable qualities.

First off, we will explore the concept of *emotion*. Psychologists generally consider a wide range of inner experiences to be emotions. On the human level, these experiences include feelings of love, fear, need, lust, jealousy, loneliness, and satisfaction. We are going to classify these feelings in a different way. Rather than refer to need and loneliness as emotions, we will lump them under the heading "emptiness." Similarly, we will lump love and satisfaction under the heading "fulfillment." The other feelings we will continue to call emotions but lump under the heading "uncertainty." Is not loneliness another word for emptiness? Is not love another word for fulfillment? Is not fear another word for uncertainty?

By cycle and threshold, the non-human organism thinks and learns abstractly. It advances from one state of comprehension to the next. Between states of comprehension, the organism experiences the growth and collapse of uncertainty. Perhaps present in a superficial way as far back as the metabolic system, or wherever one draws the line, but clearly visible in the more advanced organism, we find levels of experience that constitute forms of uncertainty—shades of uncertainty. These we will call emotions.

But our view of emotion is not the only idea that emerges from our study of the organism. Also apparent are insights into two characteristics of higher life whose explanation has always been a mystery. These are sleep and dream.

Scientists typically consider sleep to be a form of rest, and they have never offered a particularly satisfying explanation for dream. The problem is that, although sleep gives the body a chance to rest and it makes use of this time, there is little evidence to suggest that intrinsically our body needs a recuperative period. Our heart and lungs function while we sleep as does every major internal system. Yet, we find sleep rejuvenating. But if rejuvenation of the body is not the primary reason we sleep, what part of our being most benefits?

To answer this question, we return to our notion of accelerating time. In the evolution of the species, ecosystem, and biosphere, more rapid creative activity manifested in sex and lifespan. Within the organism, more rapid creative activity manifested in another mechanism to facilitate building on and creative discarding of the old, sleep and dream. In the organism, top-level creative activity is devoted to abstract thought and learning. In sleep and dream, abstract impressions realign and fall from existence unfettered by sensory input. The organism sleeps to dream and dreams to give its top-level creative process and the abstract representation of the world it maintains a chance to realign and move forward, a chance to rejuvenate.[1]

In general, when we look at the evolution of the organism, we observe that from an external point of view later, more advanced life-forms had larger brains, more complex nervous systems, and greater interaction

---

1. Sleep experts characterize the building on and creative discarding of the old that takes place when we dream as the time when the brain sorts through the short-term memories acquired during the day, discards some, and transfers others into long-term memory.

with one another and their environment. When we look at the evolution of the organism from an internal point of view, we observe that later, more advanced life-forms displayed greater awareness and individuality and more refined thought and learning. As more conscious organisms emerged, they demonstrated more pronounced emotions and periods of sleep and dream. Behavior grew increasingly free, animated, spontaneous. The individual organism developed a sense of personality. Life as we know it became more lifelike.

Thus far, we have traced life's line of consciousness through the Paleozoic and into the Mesozoic and highlighted the key internal and external features of the organism. Next, we need to take a closer look at organic evolution itself. Specifically, we must dispel certain common beliefs about evolution. We must reconcile our evolution of consciousness view with that of contemporary science, in particular with a theory called *natural selection*.

At present, it is popular to equate the event of biological evolution with the process science, at least at the moment, believes explains that event—natural selection. The two, however, are different things. Evolution is like a map. It denotes change over time, the sequence in which life-forms emerged. Natural selection is a theory. It attempts to explain how this change over time took place. In no other way are the two related.

The event of organic evolution is supported by a vast body of fossil evidence. The fossil record may not be complete in every respect, but it exists to such an extent that no reasonable mind can deny its basic message: New forms of life emerged from old forms of life. Paleontologists may not be able to tell us every detail of this emergence, but they have gathered such an abundance of evidence as to prove its existence beyond a doubt.

What about natural selection? In biology, the term "natural selection" encompasses a number of models that sprang from Darwin's original studies on evolution. The most significant are neo-Darwinism and punctuated equilibrium. Both, however, rest on, or in some way supplement, Darwin's basic view of evolutionary transformation. In the contemporary interpretation of Darwinian natural selection, mutations, or changes, are said to randomly occur in organism DNA and to create variations in organism structure. If these variations strengthen the organism, and it is better able to survive its environment and reproduce, it passes its improved DNA to its offspring. Naturally occurring genetic traits are "selected" by the environment—natural selection.

But can the simple adaptive mechanism theorized in natural selection account for the coherent evolution of species visible in the fossil record? Does Darwinism—the theoretical framework most of us have been taught to accept as a principle of nature—truly explain evolution's drive and forward direction?

To answer this question, we begin by looking at a variation of natural selection, *selective breeding*. Our ancestors bred the wolf to create the many species of dog that today offer us companionship. When studying aging, the biologist may breed a fruit fly to live longer or to reproduce in a harsher environment. In selective breeding we, rather than the environment, select characteristics to be passed to an organism's offspring. But is the external concept of "selection" the mechanism that underlies this type of organic change?

In light of our evolution of consciousness view, a more fundamental mechanism reveals itself. When we create a new breed of plant or animal, we do so not by selecting characteristics, though this may be a convenient way to think about it, but by controlling the course of the plant or animal's evolution. We manipulate the number of alternative evolutionary directions available at each juncture. We restrict the freedom of action inherent in the creative process to coax a species to over generations change form in a way we deem desirable. Even the direct manipulation of genes does nothing other than guide the unfolding of life's creative ability.

The same holds true for natural selection. From an internal standpoint, the concept of a random change in genetic structure has no meaning. Neither does the notion that desirable genetic traits are tested against the environment with the criteria for success being an organism's ability to reproduce. Organic evolution functions through the creative process. It takes place through the cycles and thresholds, the trial and error, and the creative building on and discarding of the old that from the beginning has propelled the universe to an ever more evolved state.

Natural selection is a theoretical construct that—like the big bang model of cosmic formation—attempts to explain the internal process of organic evolution through an external model. Environment selects physical traits and by doing so motivates evolution. Darwin's role in bringing the notion of organic evolution into human consciousness is remarkable, and for this we should always recognize him, among others. The event of organic evolution is a fact. But in light of a larger internal view of the universe, we must conclude that the natural selection model we thought explained that event fails to account for its existence.

Like physics and chemistry, the natural sciences face a turning point—the embracing of the internal view alongside the external. As science crosses this threshold, its need for an external model of organic evolution will end, and the theory of natural selection will fall into scientific history. It might be useful to think of certain aspects of organic function in terms of physical interaction. Epinephrine does increase blood sugar. But on the level of evolution, such relationships are a product of our indoctrination and not of reality.

I realize the extent to which the theory of natural selection has shaped contemporary thought in the natural sciences. I also realize how difficult it will be for people in the sciences, and in society, to set aside this theory. It is my hope that I have at least exposed the reader to the possibility of "life beyond Darwin." To move beyond a system of belief as entrenched as natural selection marks the crossing of a major threshold in the evolution of the scientific endeavor and humankind's vision of itself. Yet it is one that I am convinced will take place. Time will show that the human spirit will drive our quest to understand wherever the path may lead.

This thought returns us to our vision of the fundamental force behind organic change, the creative process, and positions us to further develop our internal view of evolution. An essential part of this view is the ecosystem and the biosphere.

As we mentioned, we can picture the Earth as made-up of systems of consciousness and creative activity nestled within systems of consciousness and creative activity. The level of the individual organism is wrapped within the level of the organism's social structure, which is wrapped within the level of the organism's species. This level is wrapped within the level of the ecosystem, which is wrapped within the level of the biosphere.

By cycle and threshold and by trial and error, the leading edge of the universe's creative process drove evolution forward—to build on old species and ecosystems to create new species and ecosystems. Evolution's leading arrow carried life's design to new levels of complexity and consciousness. In response, ecosystems realigned in support: Later evolutionary levels regulated the creative activity of earlier evolutionary levels. Certain species and ecosystems flourished and gave rise to new species and ecosystems. Others deteriorated and fell from existence. The net movement along evolution's trailing arrow is toward decline.

In this situation, we find the explanation for two of life's most noble qualities. As we know, the autocatalysis of consciousness that takes place with each creative cycle underlies all growth of consciousness. Inherent at every level of existence is the motivation to rise to greater awareness. On the other hand, each organism exists in support of a species, each species exists in support of an ecosystem, and each ecosystem exists in support of overall evolution. The mother wolf will fight a winter's hunger until the return of spring yet risk her life to lure an enemy from her pups. Each organism, each species, each ecosystem, and, as we will see, the biosphere itself embraces the *will to survive* and the *willingness for self-sacrifice.*

When we look at life's evolution as a creative process, we discern a pattern in the way new species emerge over time. Some species branch to create new species. Others rise unchanged through time, and still others decline and fall into extinction. Such is notable, for the branching pattern of evolution of which we speak is the pattern that is so distinctive in the fossil record. It is also the pattern we described in our chapter on cosmic formation, *figure 7.*

Last, we need to address an aspect of organic evolution we have not dealt with to a great extent but that will become a central topic in later chapters, social structure.

As organisms of greater consciousness evolved, the individual organism became more autonomous. One cell of a given type is much like another, but each crocodile is an individual. Greater consciousness makes it possible for one individual to perceive another individual as the object of its need with greater intensity and thus to form a stronger social bond. Greater autonomy generates the potential to create greater unity.

The ability to form relationships among members of a species creates a hierarchy in the evolution of social structure. Less evolved and thus less conscious and autonomous life-forms display less intricate patterns of social organization. The classic example of an organism with relatively weak social bonds and a simple social structure is the ant. In a typical ant colony, infertile worker ants gather food and build and defend the nest, and male ants impregnate the queen whose sole duty is to produce offspring. Though the colony may be large and demonstrate a division of labor, the bonds between the individual members are weak. Social structure is uniform and mechanistic.

As we move up the evolutionary ladder, this uniformity and mechanistic quality decreases. This is particularly apparent on the level of the mammal. In the bison herd, females with young form tight bands and males form their own groups. In the lion pride, adult males, females, and young maintain closely-knit subpride relationships within the highly organized pride structure. The wolf pack displays an even more complex organization comprised of parents and offspring. When we reach the level of the ape and monkey, species such as the gibbon display a rudimentary family and community structure.

More conscious organisms have the potential to create more intimate social bonds and thus to form more complex, nestled, and interwoven societies. As evolution brought increasingly advanced life into existence, the social structure this life displayed became less collective.

When we look back at life and its evolution, we are drawn to an earlier observation. The evolution of life gave rise to such diversity of species and ecosystems, to such complexity of structure and function, to such variety of behavior and social interaction, in what way other than by the creative process could we ever fundamentally account for life's nature and existence? As with the cosmos, was not the evolution of the Earth and its biosphere a manifestation of the consciousness that was the universe? Was not life the mental expression of creation?

At the end of the Mesozoic era, 65 million years ago, another wave of mass extinction swept the planet. Notable among the animals to vanish was the dinosaur. As science is inclined to do, it attributes this event to an external cause. A popular view at present is that an asteroid struck the Earth and caused massive climatic upheaval.[2] Perhaps an asteroid did strike the Earth 65 million years ago. During the four billion years of life's existence, many asteroids probably struck the Earth. But the dinosaur vanished for a less theatrical reason. Locked in evolution's trailing arrow,

---

2. Evidence of climatic upheaval at the end of the Mesozoic is visible in the geologic record as the *cretaceous-tertiary boundary*. Some paleontologists theorize that an asteroid accounted for this upheaval, others volcanic activity. The effect it had on species is also not clear. Many exposed land reptiles—lizards and crocodiles, for example—survived, whereas many protected oceangoing reptiles went extinct. Throughout the course of life's advance, there were a number of mass extinctions. One or more of these may have coincided with a geological, astronomical or other event that led to climate change. In the evolution of consciousness view, however, mass extinctions are accounted for in a fundamental way—by the creative process, by evolution's ability to build on and creatively discard the old to create the new.

such a creature was no longer needed. The age of the mammal had be-gun, and among the mammalian orders to emerge was the *primate*. Life's line of consciousness had founded the branch that would one-day lead to ourselves.

10

Reflection

B Y THE END OF the Mesozoic, the universe had set forth on a distant yet familiar evolutionary path. The Earth had entered its most recent geological era, the *Cenozoic*. This era opened on a warm world with tropical forests that spread further north and south from the equator than they do today. It was an era defined by the rise of the mammal and by the mammalian order to which we belong—the primates. The creative process had locked on the evolutionary line that would lead to life's highest organic expression—the human form.

At the beginning of the Cenozoic, several major groups dominated the mammalian class. The various species that made-up these groups consisted of relatively small creatures, few that exceeded the size of the modern bear. All were four-footed, and most had muzzles, slim heads, and five toes on each foot.

By about 54 million years ago, mammalian life had seen significant changes. The evolutionary ancestors of the horse, camel, rodent, and rhinoceros had emerged, as had the first aquatic mammals, ancestors of the modern whale. By about 38 million years ago, true carnivores had appeared—animals that resembled modern dogs and cats. By about 26 million years ago, various grazing species had evolved, as had their predators.

By about 12 million years ago, modern versions of many well-known animals inhabited the Earth. These included the elephant, mammoth, and mastodon, the latter two now extinct. Wolves had also emerged, as had the fox, lion, puma, skunk, otter, buffalo, antelope, hippopotamus, and the now vanished saber-toothed tiger.

The mammalian class also included the primates. Curiously, the first primates were small, rodentlike creatures resembling modern moles and shrews. But like all primates, they had refined vision with good depth perception and a comparatively large brain with a fissure between the first and second visual areas.

Around 50 million years ago, the primates branched into two suborders: traditionally referred to as *prosimians* and *anthropoids*.[1] The prosimians changed little over time and became the modern loris, lemur, and tarsier. The anthropoids had a more colorful evolution. By 38 million years ago, the anthropoid line itself had branched. One shoot gave rise to the new world monkey. The other gave rise to the old world monkey, gibbon, and orangutan and to a number of early apelike species.

By about 23 million years ago, one of these apelike species, a comparatively advanced creature called *Dryopithecus*, was common throughout Asia, Africa, and Europe. Within the next 15 million years, Dryopithecus, or other early apelike species, branched into the line that led to the modern gorilla and chimpanzee and into the line that led to the human being, and by about 5 million years ago, creatures distinctly human in form had emerged.[2]

Anthropologists classify these creatures in the now extinct genus *Australopithecus*, as opposed to the genus *Homo* to which we belong. Fossil remains of Australopithecus have been discovered in a number of sites in eastern and southern Africa, that continent the apparent limit of the animal's range.

The oldest of these creatures stood and walked upright and had a brain a little larger than that of a modern chimpanzee. It also had a sloping forehead, a bony ridge above the eyes, and no discernible chin. Later Australopithecus forms demonstrated slightly larger cranial capacities and teeth with more humanlike characteristics. By about 2.6 million years ago, more than five Australopithecine species lived or had lived on the African savanna. These species included Australopithecus ramidus, boisei, robustus, afarensis, and africanus. Of these species, afarensis and africanus were the most humanlike in appearance.

1. In the less popularly known taxonomic scheme used by biologists today, the order *Primate* is divided into the suborders *Strepsirrhini*, with includes lemurs and lorises, and *Haplorrhini*, which includes tarsiers, monkeys, and apes, including humans.

2. Our understanding of the human lineage is evolving and subject to interpretation. Our discussion presents the sequence of events as generally accepted at the time of the book's writing.

We will continue our account of humankind's evolutionary steps and study the species to which Australopithecus gave rise to in a moment. Before we do so, we need to tighten our focus and probe the nature of the organisms that embodied the human line.

Anthropologists study human evolution in a number of ways, two of which are most applicable to the discussion at hand. The first is through analysis of anatomical characteristics observed in or deduced from whatever fossil remains can be found. The second is through the archaeological relics created as a result of whatever activities a species may have been engaged in.

Of anatomical attributes, none is more important than those visible in the fossilized remains of the skull. More advanced species possess a more refined nervous system. Anatomically, this translates into a larger brain with respect to the animal's height and weight. Anthropologists estimate brain size by measuring the volume, or cranial capacity, of the skull. The modern chimpanzee has an average cranial capacity of about 383 cubic centimeters, or 23.4 cubic inches.[3] Australopithecus africanus had an average cranial capacity of about 450 cubic centimeters, or 27.5 cubic inches. The modern adult human being has an average cranial capacity of about 1330 cubic centimeters, or 81.2 cubic inches. As more advanced species emerged, the shape of the skull refined to accommodate a larger brain. The face flattened and the teeth and jaw decreased in size. The skull displayed a softer, less apelike appearance.

Of archeological relics, the most important left by our early ancestors were tools. The first tools were no doubt bones, stones, and sticks whose natural size and shape met certain needs. The modern chimpanzee, for example, uses slender twigs to draw termites out of their nest. The earliest tools to be substantially fabricated may have been made from wood or bone, but the oldest to survive to the present have been made from stone. The simplest of these implements is called a *chopper*. The earliest choppers date to about two million years ago and were made by striking a rounded cobble such as a palm-sized river stone with or against another rock to knock off one or more flakes. Though crude, the edge left on the original stone was sharp enough to cut meat, scrape hides, or sharpen a stick.

3. Our cranial capacity figures were taken from a number of sources. Because of differences in sample size and in methods of measurement, variations exist in the published values.

As remarkable as changes in organism anatomy and behavior were, increased brain size and the ability to make tools were nothing more than the manifestations of an underlying evolution of consciousness. As consciousness increased, our ancestors saw and interacted with their world in new ways, displayed through a growing power of abstract thought and learning.

In the last chapter, we described abstract thought as the alignment of sensory and abstract impressions to create a "state of comprehension." A couple of exercises will make this idea easier to see. We will use ourselves to conduct these exercises, but keep in mind that we are discussing thought on the prehuman level. Our early ancestors may have behaved in a more sophisticated manner than other species alive at the time; but, for reasons that will become apparent, they did not think the way you and I do.

Let us imagine we are reading the letters that make up a word, and the first letter is a "T." We recognize this letter, but it has no meaning. Let us add a couple more letters to it and create a sequence of letters: "Tei." Our mental wheels are spinning, but we still may not know what word the letters help to represent. Let us add more letters, one at a time: "Teil" and "Teilh." Now it makes sense. Given the subject matter of this book, the word must be "Teilhard." With each creative cycle, sensory and abstract impressions aligned. Finally, we crossed the threshold to a higher level of awareness, to a state of comprehension. We not only recognized the word but also grasped its meaning, a person's name. By cycle, sensory and abstract impressions align. By threshold, uncertainty collapses and lifts consciousness to a state of comprehension.

Another example would be helpful, this one a simple sentence: "Dear run away." As we read the letters that make up each word, the cycles of the creative process unfold. Sensory and abstract impressions align, and we cross the threshold to each word's meaning. But at the end of the sentence, the meaning of the words comes together in a greater way. We not only associate symbols with objects but the meaning of groups of symbols to arrive at a more complex understanding. The words lead us across a series of thresholds—from one state of comprehension to the next. Each state builds on the last to create a greater state of comprehension. We grasp a simple concept.

Now that we have reviewed our model of abstract thought and looked at it from a different angle, we need to introduce one more idea.

We can think of sensory and abstract impressions as sustained in nervous system structure of perception. Ultimately, they exist as relationships on the atomic and molecular levels. But states of comprehension are another matter. As you may recall, external manifestation results from the act of perception. A state of being is static, not associated with an external manifestation. The state of comprehension that results from the alignment of sensory and abstract impressions exists above nervous system structure of perception—as *organism consciousness*.

This observation may seem obscure even trivial, but it has the most staggering of implications. We will explore these as the chapter and book progress. For the time being, it is enough to be aware of a simple point. As abstract thought refined, the relationship between organism awareness and nervous system structure of perception changed. States of comprehension reflected an emerging separation between the organic structure of the nervous system and the top-level of organism consciousness. Though simple by modern human standards, the concept became more important than the word.

Next, we need to look at the complement to abstract thought—abstract learning. In the last chapter, we described abstract learning as an increase in consciousness, embodied in the growth and refinement of an organism's abstract representation of its world. This process can take place in three ways.

First, a portion of an organism's abstract representation will be present at birth. The organism will be born with a certain familiarity with its world and its place in that world, the necessary awareness genetically locked into nervous system structure of perception. Almost immediately out of the womb, the buffalo calf knows to stand and seek the nourishment of its mother's milk. The genetic, or *innate*, aspect of an organism's abstract representation was acquired during the period of its gestation and accounts for what we call *instinct*.

Second, learning takes place through the creative activity of the organism itself. Take the early stone toolmaker. The fabrication of even the simplest chopper requires the ability to look at the raw stone and envision a desired product. It also requires an understanding of the effect created by the blows used to create that product. To construct a tool, the early craftsman had to possess an abstract model of the stone and the characteristics of its fracture and of the tool and tool making techniques.

Through trial and error and through building on and creatively discarding the old, the early toolmaker refined his abstract representation of the world. He perfected his craft.

Third, learning takes place by way of communication. If we interpret learning as a growth in consciousness, represented by a refinement of an organism's abstract representation of its world, and thought as the creative process that brings about that growth and refinement, we can think of communication as the technique used to guide another organism's thought process. To communicate is to control the creative activity of another to enable that individual to cross the threshold to a state of comprehension. It is the technique used to help another create a comprehension of the message the messenger seeks to convey.

As organisms embodying greater consciousness emerged, the genetic, or instinctive, aspect of their make-up became less important. The worker ant goes about the task of digging a new tunnel guided largely by instinct. The behavior of the African gorilla is too flexible to be largely innate. To a greater extent, the gorilla learns its behavior through experience and through interaction with other gorillas.

This takes us back to the evolutionary line that would ultimately lead to ourselves. By about two million years ago, a new creature had emerged—one too primitive to be called human, too advanced to be called Australopithecine. Anthropologists have named this creature *Homo habilis.*

Homo habilis looked much like an Australopithecus africanus but had slightly more refined facial characteristics. It also had a larger cranial capacity, about 666 cubic centimeters on the average, or 40.6 cubic inches. Archaeologists also believe Homo habilis made the first stone tools such as the primitive chopper we described. At some point during the 300 thousand years of its evolutionary reign, it also learned to fashion a more sophisticated tool called a *biface.* Unlike a chopper, whose cutting edge is flaked on only one side, a biface is made by flaking adjacent sides to create a sharper and straighter edge. In addition, archaeologists believe Homo habilis made shelters. These ranged from simple campsites to what may have been crude huts constructed by placing stones in a ring to support upright poles or branches. Fossil and tool evidence also suggest Homo habilis hunted and scavenged a wide range of animals.

In comparison to a modern human being, Homo habilis was a primitive creature. The shape of its face and skull bear a distinct apelike quality. Yet, it had advanced to the point where most anthropologists classify it in the genus Homo.

By about 1.7 million years ago, Homo habilis had disappeared to be replaced by a creature still closer to ourselves, *Homo erectus*. Anatomically, Homo erectus was taller than Homo habilis though still shorter than a modern human being. It possessed a higher forehead, smaller teeth and jaw, and a less distinct ridge above the eyes. It had a cranial capacity that on the average measured about 950 cubic centimeters, or 58 cubic inches.

Homo erectus ranged from Asia to Africa to Europe, made a variety of choppers and bifaces as well as more sophisticated implements. These included stone awls, anvils, cleavers, scrapers, and hand-axes. Unlike in the earliest tool manufacture, where flakes had been chipped off a stone and the stone, or core, used as the tool, Homo erectus learned to use the flake as the tool, and thus was able to create a finer implement. The range of the Homo erectus toolkit also suggests that the species worked with hides and made clothing. Homo erectus lived in caves and made huts not unlike those constructed by modern hunting and gathering peoples such as the San, or African Bushman. Homo erectus also hunted big game and killed animals as intimidating as the now extinct cave bear—larger than the modern Kodiak. As significant, the species cooked its food, for it had learned to harness fire.

Perhaps the most famous Homo erectus excavation is located in a cave near the town of Choukoutien in northeast China. It was a Homo erectus skull taken from this cave in the late 1920s and commonly called "Peking Man" that Teilhard, in his role as scientific adviser to the Geological Survey of China, helped to unearth.

Between 300 and 500 thousand years ago, Homo erectus gave rise to what from an anatomical standpoint we can describe as various archaic forms of our own species, *Homo sapiens*. Groups had facial and cranial attributes that ranged from those similar to modern human beings, dating back to about 160 thousand years ago, to those closer to Homo erectus.

The best known of our archaic forms is *Homo sapiens neanderthalensis*, or Neanderthal. Anatomically, Neanderthal was as tall as we are but more robustly built, with a receding chin and a heavy brow ridge.

Interestingly, Neanderthal had a cranial capacity of about 1500 cubic centimeters, or 91.5 cubic inches—larger than that of a modern human being. During much of Neanderthal's reign, an ice age gripped the Earth. In this environment, Neanderthal bands hunted horse, reindeer, and wild cattle and scavenged mammoth and woolly rhinoceros. Neanderthal lived in caves and made a range of shelters, some from mammoth tusks draped with skins. Its tool making consisted of refinements to the basic Homo erectus toolkit with the exception of one advance, the *Levallois technique*. In this method, flake tools are chipped off a prepared core to yield a number of uniform implements. Such represented a remarkable insight into the potential of the stone. Unlike in earlier methods where the tool gradually took shape, no implement is visible until striking the single blow that leads to its production.

There is a great deal of controversy as to how to classify Neanderthal and other early Homo sapiens, and new evidence challenging traditional interpretations periodically emerges. For the sake of simplicity, we will leave the task of tracing our lineage in the period immediately following Homo erectus to the anthropologist and lump all early Homo sapiens under the heading of archaic, noting that some are anatomically more primitive than others.

Even though our archaic forms achieved certain advances, given the size of their brain and the presumed sophistication of their nervous system, outward development was quite limited. But within the archaic psyche, the anatomical complexity had evolved that would lead to a fundamental transformation of being. The creative process builds on the old to bring forth the new. The four billion years of biological evolution embodied in the archaic nervous system and its almost unimaginably complex structure of perception made possible the development that in the evolution of consciousness framework draws an unmistakable line between *humanity* and earlier human forms. The archaic psyche contained the potential transformation that would propel the universe beyond its age of life and into its next major evolutionary era, the period of advancement I call *Understanding*.

Fifteen billion years ago, the universe emerged from a primordial state of emptiness. From an internal point of view, evolution advanced across the threshold of autonomy in unity and across the threshold of design over structure. From an external point of view, it advanced through subatomic, atomic, molecular, and cosmic formation. It advanced through the development of unicellular and early multicellular life and through the structuring of the ecosystem and biosphere. It advanced through the aquatic, amphibian, reptilian, mammalian, and early primate forms. Evolution's forward edge locked in the human line. As the leading arrow of transformation thrust forward in time, our early ancestors developed a larger brain, a more complex nervous system, and a greater ability to interact with their environment and with one another. Correspondingly, they embodied a growing ability to abstractly represent and thus to comprehend their world. Thought, learning, and communication refined, and the dichotomy between states of comprehension and nervous system structure of perception grew more pronounced. Emotions refined, personality became more distinct, social structure became less collective, and periods of sleep and dream became more intense and sustained. Our early ancestors stood on the brink of becoming truly human.

And, as our ancestors poised on the brink of humanity, the universe poised on the brink of yet another evolutionary threshold. At a point in time that we will take to be about one hundred thousand years ago, uncertainty overwhelmed and collapsed. The universe turned in on itself and grasped itself as what it had become. From the standpoint of the organism, the archaic human psyche became the modern human psyche. Top-level organism consciousness no longer manifested through the alignment of sensory and abstract impressions to create states of comprehension. Top-level organism consciousness manifested through the alignment of states of comprehension to create a higher level of awareness—a level beyond that of the simple concept. Our level of abstract thought had become enwrapped within a level of awareness that existed beyond nervous system structure of perception—a level of consciousness that existed disassociated from the organic level of our being. This separation between top-level consciousness and that of our abstract and lower levels created the most profound effect. We had become a creature that was conscious of itself as if it existed removed from itself. We had become a being that was self-aware—conscious of its own consciousness. No longer did we merely know, we knew that we knew. No longer did we merely think, we pondered are ability to think. No longer did we merely learn, we understood that we learned. No longer did we merely communicate, we recognized our ability to communicate. And through the dichotomy in the human psyche—through our ability to ponder the nature of our existence—the consciousness that was creation stood face-to-face with itself. The universe crossed the threshold to *reflection*.[4]

4. The date of one hundred thousand years as the time of the universe's threshold to reflection is tentative. The advent of the human ability to think and learn reflectively is generally accepted to coincide with the appearance of hunting and funeral rites in the archeological record. Clear evidence of this dates back to ninety thousand years in Neanderthal. Evidence of more anatomically modern archaic forms, however, dates earlier, which suggests that humankind crossed the threshold to reflection earlier. For the sake of simplicity, I have chosen the round figure of one hundred thousand years as the time of this event. The reader should be aware that this date will almost certainly change as fossil and archeological evidence increases and as anthropologists learn to interpret fossil and archeological evidence as the manifestation of an underlying evolution of consciousness rather than strictly in terms of external characteristics.

PART FOUR

Understanding

11

Human Creativity

ONE HUNDRED THOUSAND YEARS ago, the universe crossed the threshold to reflection, and that threshold unfolded within the human being. Endowed with the power to reflect, humankind turned its gaze inward on itself to find itself a different creature. No longer were we merely the most intelligent animal to wander forest, tundra, and savanna. No longer were we merely the organism who walked upright and hunted with the greatest cunning of any living entity on Earth. We looked the same. Our build was stocky, our brow heavy, our chin receding. Anatomically, we were archaic. Whether we crossed the threshold to reflection in a cave overlooking a glacial valley or in a hut built along a grassland creek does not matter. Somewhere, reflection unfolded within the human being and spread to create humanity. And, in our beholding of self and world, the universe recognized its own existence. Through our power to reflect, the consciousness that was the universe gazed upon itself. And that first look at itself invoked an all-consuming desire to comprehend itself. The universe felt the need to create *meaning*.

Reflection invoked within the universe the need to understand itself and thus to create meaning. It also invoked the means to fulfill that need. With reflection, the leading edge of the universe's creative process locked in the development of human knowledge—in the advancement of human comprehension. The universe expressed its need to know through our need to know. It invoked within us the drive to understand. It embodied within every man and woman the means to build and express knowledge—the power of *human creativity*.

When we think of human creativity, we often envision its expression in the form of a painting, sculpture, or other work of art. Such artifacts represent creative efforts, but human creativity is a more fundamental quality, the essence of who we are as human beings.

All higher animals have the ability to create and store sensory and abstract impressions of life experiences and to react to situations based on these impressions. Guided by its abstract knowledge of the hunt, the timber wolf coordinates its actions with those of the pack. To chip a stone tool, the Homo erectus craftsman directed the force and angle of his blows based on his abstract knowledge of a stone's pattern of flake. The human body consists of systems of consciousness and creative activity nestled within systems of consciousness and creative activity. The threshold to reflection wrapped what was our previous top level of consciousness and creative function—that manifest as our ability to deal with the world abstractly—within a new level of consciousness and creative function, that manifest as our ability to ponder and contemplate in a deeper way, to deal with the world reflectively.

The human power to reflect is the way the creative process behaves on the top level of human consciousness. It is the manner in which building on and creative discarding of the old takes place within us. Our every higher activity—from pondering the most humble notion to solving the most intricate scientific problem to writing the greatest treatise or work of fiction—is a reflective endeavor. We were brought into being by the cycles and thresholds of the creative process and by virtue of our human nature exist as reflective beings.

Which narrows our discussion to the workings of the human creative mechanism, specifically to the facets of *reflective thought*, *reflective learning*, and *reflective communication*.

With regard to our ability to think reflectively, an exercise will help us distinguish between the creative activity that takes place on our abstract and reflective levels. As we have seen, when we read the letters that make up a word or the words that make up a simple sentence, sensory and abstract impressions align, and we cross the threshold to a state of comprehension. What happens when we read the words that make up a more evolved type of sentence?

Say the first word in our sentence is "Teilhard." We comprehend this word, but it has no greater meaning. We add words to it: "Teilhard saw the . . ." Our mental wheels spin as we reflect on the words, but there are not enough of them for us to know what thought or concept the sentence will convey. We continue to add words, one at a time: "Teilhard saw the universe as an evolution of . . ." The sentence is almost complete, and we grasp its meaning. The last word of course is "consciousness."

As our eyes scanned the sentence, two levels of creative activity were at work. On the abstract level, sensory and abstract representations aligned to create states of comprehension. On the reflective level, states of comprehension aligned until we crossed the threshold to a higher level of understanding, until we grasped the sentence's meaning.

But the idea the sentence conveyed was different from the one in last chapter's example: "Deer run away." The Teilhard sentence does not express a concept understandable on the level of abstract thought. It expresses a concept understandable on the level of reflective thought. The sentence's meaning exists only with respect to our ability to ponder the nature and meaning of our lives and our place in the universe. When we grasped the concept the sentence conveyed we crossed the threshold to a higher level of insight—to a state of reflective comprehension.

The distinction between our abstract and reflective levels becomes more pronounced when we look at the complement of reflective thought, reflective learning. As you may recall, abstract learning is a growth in consciousness manifest in the refinement of an organism's abstract representation of its world. Reflective learning is a growth in consciousness manifest in the refinement of our *reflective representation* of the world—of the framework of concepts through which we internalize and come to an understanding of our universe.

This is not to say that we human beings have lost our ability to learn abstractly, only that this ability is wrapped within our ability to learn reflectively. In the past, I spent winters teaching alpine skiing. The learning of a physical skill takes place on the abstract level. It involves the alignment of the sensory and abstract impressions needed to instill various patterns of physical movement. But our abstract, or motor, level functions in support of our conceptual level. Take a child afraid to ski and convinced the sport is too hard to learn. By way of a reassuring word or the success of a simple exercise, the instructor must show the child that his concept of inadequacy is false. To progress, the child must discard his idea of failure, built up by reflection on the possibility. Creative activity on the reflective level embraces and thus regulates and, at times, may even interfere with creative activity on the abstract level.

How, then, does our reflective representation of our world and of ourselves grow and evolve? Whereas, a portion of our abstract representation is innate, molded into nervous system structure of perception during gestation, our reflective representation is entirely acquired. This by virtue of the separation that exists between top-level human consciousness and nervous system structure of perception. Human beings have instincts such as those of the parent to protect the child, and we may reflect on and reinforce or on occasion put aside these instincts, but they exist on an abstract level. The potential to create a reflective representation becomes present at some point during our fetal development, but we create that representation ourselves.

And we do so throughout our life. With each creative cycle, states of comprehension align to create new reflective relationships. With each threshold, uncertainty collapses, and we transcend to a higher level of understanding. Driven by the need to grasp a situation, we ponder and contemplate and by doing so shape the ideas necessary to fulfill our need. We build on old thoughts and concepts to create new thoughts and concepts, and our reflective representation of the universe expands and refines to better internalize the universe.

As this takes place, old ideas reshape in support of new ideas or, if we no longer need them, fall from existence. Take the first part of this book. We began by describing the creative process step-by-step: "Emptiness drove perception of self as object which led to external manifestation and fulfillment which led to greater emptiness." As our understanding of the creative process advanced, the overall idea of the process became more important than the specifics of the creative cycle, many of which by now have no doubt slipped from our minds. Our concept of the creative process became second nature. It ingrained to the point where we could deal with it as a whole as opposed to in every detail.

But this is not to say that old ideas always fall away without effort. Like the species that fights extinction or the writer who finds it painful to delete parts of a manuscript, we at times struggle to abandon obsolete notions. In the sixteenth century, Nicolaus Copernicus fought to convince the world that the Earth revolved around the sun. In 1887, it took Albert Michelson and Edward Morley's failed experiment to determine the Earth's velocity through space to convince a reluctant scientific community that light did not travel through the ether. At this moment, are we struggling to set aside the concept that the only proper way to deal with the universe is in the purely external terms embraced by present-day science?

It is natural to feel a reluctance to abandon long held ideas, and prudence in doing so is an admirable quality. Yet, we at times reach a point where our attachment to old ideas hinders our evolution. We arrive at this state when we use our creative ability to justify ideas for no other reason than they may once have been worthwhile. We can think of the process whereby we direct the power of our creativity to maintain concepts beyond their usefulness and thus to stall evolution as *stagnation*. Within the individual, stagnation reveals itself as insecurity and as the ego that results when we too tightly associate our sense of self with beliefs kept alive beyond their time. Within humanity, stagnation reveals itself as dogma, racism, ethnocentrism, and fundamentalism. Stagnation is the antithesis of evolution—the *dark side of the creative force*. By virtue of our autonomy, we have the power to align our thoughts and actions in support of the universe's greater creative endeavor. We also have the power to hinder that endeavor.

This brings us to an issue most of us will face during our lives. The difficulty we experience building on and creatively discarding old ideas tends to increase as we age. Many individuals, young and old but old in particular, are locked in a rigid view of life and universe. They seem at a loss to deal with the pace and flexibility that characterizes certain aspects of contemporary existence. But, we must ask, is such a decline of creative function unavoidable?

On the abstract and lower levels of body consciousness, a slowdown of creative activity is innate, a result of the lifespan programmed into our genetic makeup. We may be able to forestall this decline through diet, exercise, and healthy living, but some degree of degradation is inevitable. The eighty-year-old cannot learn to ski as quickly or as well as the twelve-year-old.

But we must not forget that in our view the top level of human consciousness exists removed from the organic level. As we age, the connection between our abstract and reflective levels may weaken and thus reduce our ability to express our thoughts and to interact with the world. But our top level of creative activity exists above these limitations, potentially as functional as ever, more so due to the decades of experience ingrained in our reflective representation of the world. The crime against ourselves is to deny this creativity—to close our minds to the world, to see ourselves as other than vital. To do so is to truly grow old.

Reflective thought and learning are the core of human creativity. Yet, none of us lives alone in the universe. This brings us to the topic of communication. Reflective learning is the growth and refinement of our reflective representation of the universe. Reflective thought is the process that brings about that growth and refinement. Reflective communication is the tool that guides another person's thought process, the mechanism that stirs another person's creativity.

Central to the mechanism of communication is language. In anthropological circles, the question as to what constitutes language fuels a great deal of speculation. When we shift our view to the internal, this question evaporates. We see language—spoken, written, mathematical, and otherwise—as a medium of interaction, as a way to guide the creative activity of another. As such, artistic expression is a form of language. True works of art—the greatest paintings, buildings, sculptures, songs and symphonies—speak to us. They tell a story. Before reflection, the vocal and other signals used to invoke a creative response represented language on the abstract level. After reflection, they represented language on the reflective level. Language is not a development that we or any other species by chance invented. It is an aspect of creative function. As we evolve to greater awareness, language evolves to allow us to express that awareness.

Why then are our verbal and other language skills sometimes effective in communicating our ideas and sometimes not effective? We all remember struggling to grasp a concept we read about in a high school or college textbook. Likewise, we all remember struggling to pay attention in a class or lecture. Why do we find certain applications of language more difficult than others?

In traditional teaching approaches such as the lecture and textbook, teachers and writers present concepts linearly, one after the other. Later concepts may build on earlier concepts, but the development of ideas takes place without the element of "need." It is a rare teacher that nurtures a student's desire to learn. The student may feel compelled to pay attention in class to pass an exam, but such a motivation is distant, not directly associated with the task at hand. Linear methods of communication do not mesh with the dynamic, curvilinear pattern of change that characterizes the creative process. They do not effectively interact with and thus stimulate that process. Often times, teachers and other educators simply fail to spark our interest.

The most effective method of communication would be the one that most directly interacts with another person's creative activity. The best example of this method is the *story*.

Story structure reflects the pattern of change associated with the creative process and thus is effective in guiding that process. *Figure 9* makes this relationship easier to see. Every successful story, from that told in the most probing novel to that told in the most superficial movie, begins by invoking a need within the reader or viewer. This part of the story is called the *complication*. Here the story's main character faces some obstacle that she must overcome by the end of the story, and we face the need to see how the character overcomes that obstacle.

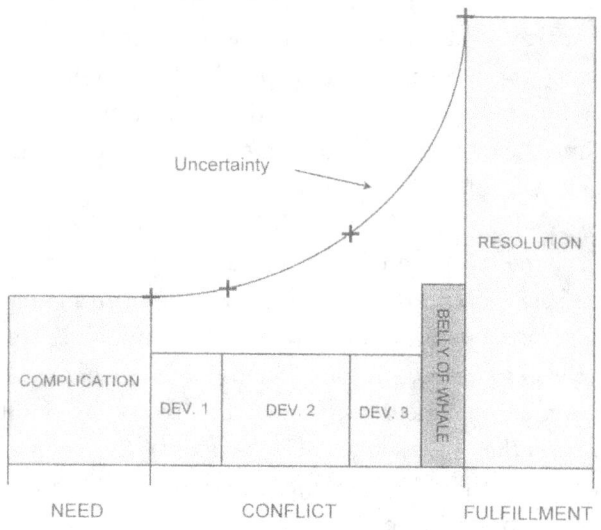

Fig. 9. Story Structure. The story is the form of communication whose structure most closely relates to the creative process. The graph plots uncertainty, or story tension, as it builds between the story's complication and resolution.

Following the complication, a story will usually progress through three *developments*, the minimum number needed to generate the growth curve characteristic of the creative process. Each development climaxes in a minor threshold and represents the trial and error and the increase in consciousness and uncertainty experienced by the story's main character. Each development opens the door for the story's complication to be resolved but at the same time makes it increasingly difficult for the character to achieve that resolution.

At the end of the third development, uncertainty grows to the point where it overwhelms the story's main character. Yet, when all is darkest, uncertainty collapses and light shines through. The story's main character grasps the nature of the story's complication and by doing so crosses a threshold to the understanding she needs to, in the story's final part, the *resolution*, overcome the obstacle she originally faced.

Not every story employs this simple structure, but all employ some variation. The "saga," for example, consists of a number of smaller stories nestled within an overall complication and resolution. To be effective, every story must create within the reader or viewer the need to see how the story will work out in the end and then guide the reader or viewer to create what the author intended to be the fulfillment of that need.

Another way to describe the story was put forth by the twentieth century American anthropologist *Joseph Campbell* in his studies of culture and mythology. Campbell noted that story structure has changed little over time and is essentially the same in every society. This we would expect given the fundamental nature of the creative process.

In Campbell's model, the story's complication takes place when the story's main character, or hero, crosses what Campbell calls the "threshold to adventure." Here the hero leaves home to set forth on a journey through a world where he is helped and tested by people and forces along the way. Ultimately, the hero reaches the point in his journey where all hope is lost. There, at the moment uncertainty overwhelms—at the point Campbell calls the "*belly of the whale*"—darkness transforms into light and the hero crosses a second threshold to gain the knowledge, or undergo the "expansion of consciousness," he needs to make his way home.

In his return journey, the hero may literally or symbolically undergo "*resurrection*" from death to, when he finally reaches his home, discover he has undergone a rebirth of his being. He finds that he embodies the transformation between "*two worlds.*"

Not all forms of communication lend themselves to story structure. But the more we incorporate the principle of need, development, and fulfillment into our communication, the better we can guide another person across the threshold to understanding.

Which concludes our look at reflective thought, reflective learning, and reflective communication and propels our discussion to an even more provocative level—to the role of human creativity in evolution. What is the relationship between the individual and the creative endeavor of humanity and between humanity and the creative endeavor of the universe?

To understand this, we must drop from our view the image of physical creation. We must blot from before our eyes the picture of our bodies and of the Earth and heavens. Throughout our depiction of evolution, we have characterized progress as the emergence of more conscious and autonomous evolutionary forms within the unity of a more conscious and autonomous universe. The universe's threshold to reflection elevated this line of evolutionary advance to a fundamentally new level.

Prior to the moment when the universe embraced reflection, all evolutionary forms were composed of earlier evolutionary forms. Atoms are made of subatomic particles. Molecules are made of atoms, cells are made of molecules, and organisms are made of cells. The threshold to reflection marked a turning point in this developmental pattern, an evolutionary breach.

On its top level, human consciousness embodies an internal model of the universe made-up of states of comprehension—states not sustained in nervous system structure of perception, states that exist as disassociated consciousness. Our level of reflective consciousness interacts with our level of abstract consciousness and thus with all lower body levels but exists removed from these levels. By virtue of our ability to reflect, we account for the distance within ourselves we experience. By virtue of our human creativity, we account for the separation of the psyche—the world we sustain within our being. Our creative activity generates the substance of our internal world. The time-space existence we experience within ourselves is the external manifestation produced by the cycles and thresholds of our top-level creative process. We create and exist within an orb of personal time and space, a construct relative to our own being.

Reflection marked the emergence of entities so consciousness that on their reflective level they existed removed from prior evolutionary forms—so aware that they existed independent of earlier structure of perception. With reflection, the universe existed as an entity of consciousness made-up of human beings, entities so autonomous as to experience as isolated their top-level of being—entities so aware as to be universes in themselves.

Is this not to be expected? In our view of evolution, the universe began with an expansion of consciousness followed by the formation of autonomous entities of consciousness within itself. These entities perceived one another as object and, by doing so, created more complex and conscious entities. With the metabolic system, structure achieved the complexity for an aspect of consciousness to perceive itself as the object of its need and thus to fully sustain its own creative process. It follows that this trend of increasing autonomy must lead to aspects with the consciousness to, in part, exist as universes within the greater construct of creation.

Moreover, as the threshold to reflection created a dichotomy between the human being's reflective and pre-reflective levels, it created a dichotomy between the universe's reflective and pre-reflective levels. The structure of perception that underlies all prior evolution and all that we take to be the physical universe fell into the realm of evolution's trailing arrow.

Why, we ask when we face a tornado or other natural disaster, would "God" do this to us? Just as we have little conscious control over our heart rate, blood pressure, and other embedded levels of creative activity, the universe's existence on the reflective level would have little conscious control over creative activity on earlier evolutionary stages. Local creative activity dictates patterns of subatomic, atomic, molecular, cosmic, geological, and climatological behavior. Floods, tornadoes, hurricanes, and earthquakes result from long established trailing-arrow patterns of physical interaction and not from the willful acts of a creator.

The dichotomy between the universe's reflective and pre-reflective levels brings us to a conclusion that is difficult to fathom but that as we think about it we take to be inescapable. With the threshold to reflection, the consciousness that was the universe disassociated from the mental construct of prior evolution. With the threshold to reflection, the consciousness that was the universe rose above the mental fabric of its gestation and stood before itself and all that it had created as an entity of reflective consciousness on its own.

As such, we, on our highest level, and the universe, on its highest level, exist as autonomous beings connected by a reflective structure of perception. The top-level of awareness experienced by the human being exists removed from the sphere of humanity and from the greater consciousness of universe but at the same time embraces humanity and the greater consciousness of the universe. The top-level of the universe's consciousness exists removed from the sphere of humanity and the human being but at the same time embraces humanity and the human being. Through the power of our autonomy, by the cycles and thresholds of our creative process, we create relationships between one another and between the universe. The universe—through the power of its autonomy and by the cycles and thresholds of its creative process—creates relationships between itself, humanity, and the human being. Humanity and the universe exist within a construct of interaction—a structure of reflective perception.

At work in this heightened construct of interaction is the universe's overall creative process—its forward arrow thrust to greater understanding. Consciousness, manifest as knowledge, generates within the individual—catalyzed by the individual's interaction with others and in conjunction with the consciousness that is universe. For this reason, an insight may strike more than one person at the same time. We communicate our understanding until it embraces humanity and, through humanity's assimilation, is internalized by the universe.

This brings us to a point that touches our lives in a personal way. The individual in whom evolution's forward arrow momentarily embeds may be an Aristotle, Copernicus, Galileo, Newton, Bohr, Einstein, or Teilhard, but it need not be such a figure. Humanity progresses on many levels. Understanding has nooks and crannies. Every human being can and in some way does contribute to humankind's forward movement. We are united by the role we play in the endeavor of the universe's evolution. "A truth once seen, even by a single mind," Teilhard wrote, "always ends up by imposing itself on the totality of human consciousness."[1]

The individual exists within and independent of the greater movement of humanity. Humanity exists within and independent of the greater movement of the universe. To create understanding is to create consciousness. By way of creative building on and discarding of the old, consciousness evolves within the individual and spreads to lift humanity to greater awareness. As humanity evolves to greater awareness, so evolves the reflective outcome of the fifteen billion years of creative becoming that we call the universe. In the reflective structure of perception that associates humanity with creation, we are the leading edge of time's progression. Our lives define the forward arrow of evolution's advance. The cycles and thresholds of the universe's overall creative process unfold within us.

Some one hundred thousand years ago, the universe crossed the threshold to reflection. With the ability to reflect came an overpowering sense of curiosity. The universe felt the need to understand the nature and purpose of its existence—the drive to grasp the reason for its being. Reflection also brought the power to fulfill that need—human creativity,

1. Teilhard de Chardin, *The Phenomenon of Man*, 218.

the ability to ponder and contemplate, the capacity to create, refine, and express notions of how and for what purpose it came to be. Driven by the need to understand, empowered with the means, the consciousness that was creation entered a new stage in its evolution. With the forward arrow of its overall creative process locked in the advancement of human understanding, the universe set forth on yet another phase of its journey to perfection—the endeavor to create meaning.

12

Belly of the Whale

IMAGINE WE ARE AT that moment one hundred thousand years ago when the universe set forth to create meaning—at that instant when the first human being crossed the threshold to reflection. Who was that first reflective person? What might his or her life have been like? Did he or she feel alone, different, an oddity among the members of the group? Endowed with an awareness of his or her consciousness, that first human being had the ability to reflect and question, the means to grapple with his or her differences. But soon others must have come to the power of reflection. Perhaps these individuals traveled from band to band and sought out one another. Perhaps they nurtured reflection within their own social units. The details we may never know, but groups of reflective individuals did form. And the behavior they displayed, revealed through the archeological record they left, marked the beginning of a human endeavor that would carry us from huts and caverns to computers and skyscrapers. It would also carry us to a growing presence in the universe of the "dark side of the creative force."

When the universe crossed the threshold to reflection, the forward arrow of its overall creative process moved beyond organic evolution. Never again would the Earth's biosphere embody the diversity of species and ecosystems that had once flourished. Evolution's leading shoot locked in the human being, in the advance of human understanding, in as Teilhard called it "Noogenesis." As a result, our ancestors acted in new and remarkable ways.

In what is now Italy, we ventured into the depths of a cave to hurtle clay pellets at a stalagmite that to this day resembles an animal. Elsewhere, we collected cave bear skulls, arranged them in cavern nooks, and put them in pits and stone chests. We also buried our dead. We laid to rest the bodies of our companions, placing food, animal remains, and flint tools at their sides. On their graves, we set stones, spread ocher, and arranged flowers.

Hunting and funeral rites reveal a new experience of existence. Long had the human species observed the migration of game, the passing of seasons, and the cycles of plant growth. Never had we asked what forces directed these movements and never had we sought to appeal to these forces. Long had the human species felt an awareness of a consciousness that in some way touched all others—of the consciousness we call the universe. Never had we contemplated our feeling of this awareness. Long had the human species known death. Never had we pondered death and sought to relate it to the separation we felt within our being.

Confronted with their world, our ancestors attempted to explain what they saw and felt in many ways. They observed patterns of natural movement and events in their lives and attributed such to the action of conscious entities removed from themselves. To our ancestors, beings controlled the migration of game, the passing of day into night, birth and death, and the mishaps and moments of good fortune that take place in every person's life. Did they envision these beings in their own image? Did they question the relationship between these beings and their experience of the greater consciousness that we call the universe?

Our ancestors also sought to explain the behavior of their world by attributing such to physical interaction. Rain makes the rivers rise. Snow drives the deer from the hills. Fire burns one's flesh and cooks one's food. The period that followed the threshold to reflection was a time when the most fundamental human ideas were in the formative stages. Our notion of a god or gods took shape, as did our notion of a soul and afterlife. We devised the earliest systems of spiritual belief and the earliest ways to predict and manipulate the behavior of our environment. We founded the rudiments of what would one day become organized science, religion, and engineering.

As we would expect, however, the initial manifestation of the transformation in our psyche was also in many ways limited. We buried our dead, but in shallow graves and with little ritual. We practiced hunting rites, but none that were elaborate. Artistic expression in our tools and artifacts existed, but was minimal. As we groped to deal with what we had become, human anatomy restructured in support. Our vocal apparatus refined to allow for the expression of more intricate language. The nervous system complexity that had made it possible for us to cross the threshold to reflection was no longer needed, and the brain shrank from its archaic to its modern proportions. By about forty thousand years ago, our transition to a reflective way of life was complete. Archaic human-kind had in every respect become modern humankind; and, but for a dwindling number of comparatively advanced Neanderthal bands that roamed for a few more millennia, our earlier forms no longer populated the Earth. Men, women, and children physically no different from our-selves inhabited the plains and forests—people who in every sense were Homo sapiens sapiens. This development marked the beginning of a new period in our evolution. "Hominisation," as Teilhard defined humankind's evolution to greater humanness, took place at a more rapid rate.

Our clearly modern ancestors carved figurines from stone and deco-rated spear shafts with geometric patterns. They wore fitted cloths and adorned their bodies with rings, bracelets, and necklaces made from ivory. The stone tools they manufactured not only demonstrated functionality but also an aesthetic quality, a display of artisanship beyond necessity and that varied from region to region and from toolmaker to toolmaker. Our ancestors made ornaments from bones and shells and built shelters and ritual structures from wood, tusks, and skins.

They also painted animals on cave walls. Perhaps no other early archeological relic has captured our attention more than cave art. This form of expression dates back as far as forty thousand years and has been found at sites throughout the world. The most famous of these sites are in Western Europe. Paintings in the caves at Lascaux France depict deer, bear, horse, and other animals. One shows a dying hunter and a wounded bison, the first known dramatic narrative expressed in visual form. Most early cave paintings were made using pigments concocted by mixing ocher and other colored earths with animal fat. The pigment was applied with the fingers or with fur, moss, and sticks. Images may also have been made by pulverizing charcoal and other pigments and blowing them onto the stone using a hollow tube.

Our early ancestors created a world rich in gods and spirits, rites and artistic expression. In this world, they experienced loneliness, uncer-tainty, and fulfillment. They formed groups, nurtured sons and daughters, mourned the death of loved ones, and speculated on the passage into afterlife. Driven by the need to understand, our early ancestors learned from those around them and through the trial and error of their own reasoning. They sought to communicate with the gods they believed controlled their world and asked for knowledge and a better life.

By about thirty thousand years ago, humankind had migrated through Indonesia to inhabit Australia and within the next fifteen thousand years across the Bering Strait and along the banks of the northern ice flows to inhabit North and South America. By about twelve thousand years ago, human progress had swung in a fundamentally different direction. The development took place that marked the beginning of a still more advanced period in our evolution. Humankind moved away from the nomadic, hunting and gathering subsistence pattern it had inherited from its archaic ancestors and began to cluster in the first permanent settlements.

To understand the motivation behind humankind's creation of an urban environment, we need to revisit our idea of social structure. As human understanding increased, the individual became more conscious and autonomous. Our greater awareness made it possible for us to perceive one another as the object of our need with greater intensity and thus to create stronger social bonds. The family became more important, and bands joined to form larger communities. Spurred by the growing complexity of our social interactions, we found it desirable, albeit essential, to live in permanent settlements. In the evolution of consciousness view, urbanization was an outgrowth of life's four-billion-year-old trend toward less collective social structure.

Where, then, did the first communities spring up and what might they have looked like? At one time, anthropologists believed urbanization began at a single spot called the "nuclear area" of Mesopotamia, located in present day Iraq, then diffused throughout the Near East, spread north into the Indus valley and China, westward into Europe, and across the Bering Strait into the Americas. Today, most scientists feel urbanization arose independently at these and other locations. In either view, the first settlements were little more than areas where people stayed for extended periods during their wanderings. These places may have been caves or clusters of shelters built near a stable source of food and water or near an area with religious significance. As time progressed, life increasingly revolved around these settlements. People felt the need to live closer and chose to make the settlements their permanent home.

The greater number of individuals in the urban settlement and the close proximity between individuals had a remarkable effect on evolution. In contrast to the isolation experienced by a member of a nomadic band, the city dweller could interact with a larger segment of humanity. In an urban setting, people could more readily exchange ideas and stories and pass them from generation to generation. City life was an outcome of time-acceleration, a catalyst in our endeavor to understand. If we were to imagine the Earth of twelve thousand years ago in terms of human awareness and creative activity, we would see it as a vast globe, most of which was dark. Yet, scattered in this darkness, bright spots would catch our eye. Such would denote areas of heightened reflection, the location of the first settlements.

In addition to the evolutionary function of the urban community, city life had many ramifications, some so significant as to affect virtually every generation that came after and, even today, profoundly influence our view of the world.

At the root of these consequences is one unavoidable outcome of the early permanent settlement. Before urbanization, human bands had occupied the same basic ecological niche for millions of years. As nomadic hunters and gatherers, we maintained a relationship with our environment not unlike that of any other species in an ecosystem. Groups may have experienced hunger as ecosystems realigned, but for the most part the plains and jungles provided for their needs. When we moved into settlements, we broke away from this environmental relationship. Only a limited amount of game could be hunted and fruits and tubers gathered within a reasonable distance from the settlement. As a result, the early urban community experienced a chronic need for food and other goods. It existed in a state of intrinsic *scarcity of recourses*.

Scarcity of resources spurred the development of systems to coordinate the way people gathered food and other commodities in the countryside, where they existed in surplus, and to transport them into the city, where they existed in deficit. Urbanization founded *scarcity-based economics*, an economic philosophy based on the notion that resources are by nature limited and human material wants are by nature unlimited and that some mechanism must exist to encourage the production of goods and to regulate their allocation.

Moreover, urbanization and scarcity-based economics transformed our view of the world. For the first time, we did not see ourselves as part of our environment; we saw ourselves as separate from and in opposition to our environment. Our lives were a struggle to eke out of the Earth what we needed to feed, cloth, and shelter ourselves and our community. Urbanization and scarcity brought into human consciousness the concept of nature—the idea that we are separate from the natural world. In a larger sense, urbanization and scarcity nurtured humanity's ideals of wealth and property, of survival, competition, and economically based social structure.

As significant, urbanization and scarcity spurred the rise of agriculture. As a city's population increased, it reached the point where the demand for resources outstripped the supply provided by natural ecological systems in the vicinity. This led to the use of techniques where a greater amount of food could be taken from a smaller area of land. Here we must dispel a common belief. Anthropologists once thought that farming was the invention, or "basic adaptation," that made urbanization possible. As we would expect, archeological evidence suggests otherwise. Excavations in Iraq, for example, indicate that the first settlements were established about eleven thousand years ago, a thousand years before the first evidence of sustained food production in the region. Even our archaic ancestors probably understood the concept of plant germination, but they had no reason to apply it. Why grow food when you can pick it up in your wanderings? Agriculture did not lead to urbanization. Rather, it made it possible for us to sustain urban growth and our drive to create a less collective society.[1]

By about six thousand years ago, humankind had undergone still another leap forward in its evolution to greater knowledge and understanding. Humanity had advanced beyond the realm of the prehistoric and set forth into the age of recorded history.

As one might expect, two developments marked this turning point. First, we invented writing and began to record our fears, thoughts, aspirations, and the events of the day. Second, we invented methods of calculation and began to compute time, weight, and distance.

The earliest known writing is attributed to the Sumerians of Mesopotamia and was a "logographic" system, or one in which a symbol represents a complete word. A short time later, writing emerged in Elam

---

1. At some point prior to urbanization, our ancestors domesticated animals, in particular dogs and sheep, and incorporated herding into their nomadic way of life. As nomadic peoples, we also made use of certain elements of agriculture, for example the scattering of seeds so that plants could take root by the time we returned. The stationary production of crops, however, began after urbanization.

and Egypt. The Egyptian system was based on hieroglyphics, or pictorial symbols that represent recognizable objects. The Elamite system was "logo-syllabic," or a method of writing where symbols are used to represent sounds as opposed to complete words. Writing developed at a later date in the Aegean, Anatolia, the Indus Valley, and China.

Inseparable from the advent of writing, mathematics is a language that makes it possible for us to compare two or more quantities. These quantities may be as varied as the lengths of the three sides that make up a triangle and the amounts of tin and copper needed to formulate bronze. Like writing, anthropologists believe mathematics originated in the Middle East. The first mathematical systems included two methods of symbolism and calculation: the Egyptian system and the Babylonian system. At their onset, both methods were limited to arithmetic and geometry. As time progressed, they expanded to include simple algebra. Later, the Greeks built on elements of both systems to invent an abstract mathematics founded on a structure of axioms, proofs, and definitions.

Mathematics facilitated economic transaction. It also made it possible for us to predict seasonal, astronomical, and other reoccurring patterns of natural movement with great precision and to develop the physics, chemistry, and engineering needed to advance metallurgy and construction. Writing made it possible for us to record this and other knowledge. Together, writing and mathematics were the tools that enabled humanity to expand its knowledge beyond the limits placed on it by oral tradition. They were the catalysts, the twin developments that opened the way for human understanding to evolve at a vastly accelerated rate.

And, in the centuries that followed, the accelerated rate at which human understanding emerged led to a never before seen outpouring of creative expression and creative forms.

About 4,700 years ago, we constructed the first monumental works of religious architecture built in stone. This development primarily took place along the Nile River and included Djoser's Temple and the Step Pyramid at Saqqara and the pyramid complex at Giza. There, the Great Pyramid of Khufu stood some 146 meters, or 480 feet, high and contained as many as 2.3 million stone blocks that on the average weighed 2.5 metric tons each.

About 3,500 years ago, the development of human understanding marked a philosophical advance. *Polytheism*, the notion that multiple gods controlled various aspects of the world, began to shift to *monothe-*

ism, the notion that a single god controlled all aspects of the world. The advent of monotheism is attributed to the Egyptian ruler Akhenaton, who established the belief that the "sun god" was the all-embracing spirit of the universe. Monotheism brought with it the idea of an all knowing, all-powerful, and thus a never changing god. Today, such a vision of the divine spirit underlies or has a place in every major system of religious belief.

By the time monotheism had entered the human experience, social structure had advanced beyond that displayed in the first urban settlements. Communities had united to form cities, and cities had aligned to create states. States had united to create nations, and nations had aligned to create still more complex social structures. At the height of its development, about 3,400 years ago, the Egyptian Empire, arguably the world's first multi-national state, encompassed a diversely organized population distributed over some 400,000 square miles.

The consciousness of a citizen living in the Egyptian Empire not only encompassed his community but reached out to embrace a vast geographical area. If we were to imagine the Earth at that time in terms of human creativity, we would no longer see it as a dark globe dotted with an occasional bright spot. Many bright spots in the new and old worlds would catch our eye, each denoting a concentration of human awareness. From these points, rays would emanate, linking one urban area to another and marking humanity's inkling as to the scope of its Earth.

About 2,300 years ago, the shift in thought that we discussed in the first chapter took place. Humankind began to think of its world as existing on two levels, the internal and the external. In many respects, this break in viewpoint acted as a catalyst in our development. It allowed us to focus our creative efforts on unraveling the mysteries of the physical world.

Eighteen hundred years ago, we invented paper. Eleven hundred years ago, we harnessed waterpower to drive the first simple industry. Seven hundred years ago, we began the large-scale production of gunpowder. In 1486, Bartolomeu Dias navigated the Cape of Good Hope. In 1520, Ferdinand Magellan began the first circumnavigation of the Globe. In 1543, Nicolaus Copernicus proposed an astronomical system in which the planets revolved in circular orbits around the sun. Three hundred years ago, Galileo founded the principles of the scientific method, and Isaac Newton formulated the classical equations to describe gravity and motion.

By the time of the industrial revolution in the mid 1700s, Western culture dominated the human experience. In the Western view, those of a religious bent saw the human being as of a divine origin, defined by the existence of a soul. Those of a scientific bent saw the human being as a machine, complex but mechanical nonetheless. We lived in a world characterized by competition for material resources and by competition between two outwardly irreconcilable worldviews. A perplexing relationship existed between the lofty aims of religion and the use of those aims to achieve the worldly goals of power and material acquisition.

Into this atmosphere of economic and ideological conflict, the notion of organic evolution took root, and the man most responsible for its development, Charles Darwin, was born. What now seems clear is that in his attempt to explain the process of organic evolution, Darwin took the views of his culture, namely those of competition and a struggle to survive, and imposed those views on his observations of the natural world. In 1859, Darwin published his *On the Origin of Species*. The mechanistic view of life and of the human being had prevailed.

In 1876, Alexander Graham Bell patented the telephone. In 1898, Marie Curie discovered radium. In 1905, Albert Einstein published his special theory of relativity. In 1913, Neils Bohr hypothesized his model of atomic structure. In 1914, an assassin gunned down Archduke Francis Ferdinand of then Austria-Hungary, and humankind entered its first World War. In 1915, Einstein proposed his general theory of relativity. By 1927, quantum mechanics had achieved a high degree of development. In 1939, Adolf Hitler invaded Poland, and humankind entered its second World War. On July 16, 1945, the United States exploded the first atomic bomb in a test at Alamogordo, New Mexico.

As humanity rose from the rubble of worldwide conflict and gazed on the devastation it had unleashed on itself, it did so with new eyes. Our struggle and progress during the first half of the twentieth century had elevated humankind to a new level of awareness. Never again would the human being see itself as isolated in the world. We felt within ourselves a new connection to one another. We experienced a state of global consciousness.

Teilhard's notion of the "*noosphere*" will help us understand this state. When we think of the Earth, it is possible to speak of a lithosphere, or the layer of hard rock that makes up the Earth's crust. It is also possible to speak of a hydrosphere and of a biosphere, or the Earth's lakes and oceans and the layer of living things they support. We can also speak of a noosphere, or a layer composed of human thought and the activities and artifacts that result from that thought. The World Wars and the progress they fueled had elevated the human being to an awareness of his or her place in the human community and with respect to the Earth's natural and political geography. Evolution had enabled humankind to internalize the noosphere. If we were to imagine the Earth after the Second World War in terms of human awareness and creative activity, we would see it as enwrapped within a radiant orb strewn with spots and regions of intense brightness, each linked to all others by glowing strands of consciousness.

Today, this web of human awareness manifests through a vast information industry—a pervasive media, educational, and communication network. We witness the cycles and thresholds and the trial and error of the human endeavor as they unfold. Our knowledge reaches out to embrace atomic, molecular, cosmic, and organic structure. We have probed the heavens, mapped the evolution of life, and deciphered the history of civilization. We have created the scientific and engineering framework to reshape our world in almost any way we imagine.

Here our story of humanity and the universe enters the twenty-first century and, as we began the chapter by stating, faces a growing presence in the universe of the dark side of the creative force. As remarkable as human progress has been, we seem loath to realize that such is the outcome of a greater evolution. As we ponder the universe, we question our ability to grasp the meaning of our existence. As we reflect on our accomplishments in the noosphere, we fail to ask to what end will all that we have made and learned enable us to achieve? Humanity confronts the entrenchment of the obsolete—the peril of a stagnant ideal of creation.

When taken in its entirety, the evolution of consciousness view thrusts us beyond our present understanding of who we are and of the nature of our existence. In doing so, it also draws us to a conclusion about the universe's future and our present moment in the unfolding of that future. We realize that the age of understanding has reached its climax. We confront the possibility that the universe is today undergoing the most fundamental shift in evolutionary direction since the transcendence to reflective consciousness more than a thousand lifetimes ago.

And, like the turning point to reflection, the crossing of this threshold is taking place within us. By virtue of the reflective structure of perception that defines the relationship between humanity, the human being, and the consciousness that is the universe, we mark the forward thrust of evolution's arrow. As we have since the creative process locked in the advancement of the human line, we define the leading edge of the universe's advance. Evolution's cycles, thresholds, and creative building on and discarding of the old unfold within us.

As such, the uncertainty associated with the crossing of an evolutionary threshold masses within the human community. In our endeavor to create meaning, the noosphere has become so full of data piled on data, of knowledge piled on knowledge, of information piled on information that the universe's age of understanding is bursting at the seams. We feel lost, alienated, swept along in a torrent of empty facts and inapplicable information—overwhelmed by the social, personal, military, political, economic, and environmental consequences.

In our quest for meaning, we grope from path to path, from leader to leader, from ideology to ideology. At every turn in our meandering, we face the embedded old: stagnant religious, economic, scientific, and academic ideals and practices. We feel locked, trapped, stifled, held in irons by the limited vision of those who run our institutions and governments. We confront a world that has yet to mass the courage to look with open eyes into the future, a universe gripped by the views and philosophies of the past, clutched in the nether of what has been.

The value of knowledge lies not in knowledge or in the extent to which we can accumulate it but in our ability to put what we know to use—in our capacity to build on our insight to advance to a higher evolutionary state. We yearn to know but despite the world's banks of data fail to grasp the significance of our existence. We long to internalize but despite the world's religious and scientific edifices fail to comprehend the purpose for our being. In the story of the universe and its evolution, humanity finds itself at the dark moment before a transformation—as Joseph Campbell would characterize it, adrift in the belly of the whale.

13

Meaning

TODAY, TRADITIONAL WAYS TO create fulfillment in our lives seem little more than dreams of stability and belonging in a world driven by economic power and by factions in political, military, and subversive opposition—fantasies of contentment in a universe rushing to some ill-defined future. We wonder what life will be like in the years ahead and fear for our freedom and for the world we are creating for our children. In a way whose experience is unique for every human being, the dark cloud of uncertainty envelops the planet. The question we now ask is how dark must this cloud grow before we cross a threshold and evolve beyond the universe's age of understanding. To what depths must uncertainty tear into the fabric of our well-being before we move on? How deep within the belly of the whale must the human experience sink, and how strongly must the whale's belly churn, before we rise above?

Our need for insight compels us to reflect on the present state of the universe. We begin by looking at the two towers of human intellectual achievement that with regard to their nature and origins we have spoken about before—science and religion.

As we have discussed, science evolved as the mechanism that we use to explain and control the physical universe. Because of the great strides science has made toward achieving this end, it has reached the point where today it operates on two levels.

On one hand, science is the tool that underlies basic research. It is the process we engage in to answer questions posed by medicine, engineering, and other applied disciplines. How much steel reinforcement do we need in a concrete beam to enable that beam to support a given load? What voltage must we apply to a circuit to overcome the resistance created by a series of components? What causes cancer, tuberculosis, and other disorders and how can we intervene to prevent these diseases? So effective is science in addressing questions such as these that, when properly administered, it is hard to imagine a more finely honed implement of inquiry. In its role as the instrument of research, science does what it has evolved to do. It maps physical behavior.

On the other hand, science is the tool we turn to in our quest to unravel the greater mysteries of the universe, namely those of the universe's origin and elemental composition. During the first half of the twentieth century, science seemed well on its way to solving these mysteries. Theorists whose lives overlapped with many of our own invented models to predict the behavior of matter on levels as far ranging as the cosmic, the genetic, and the subatomic and devised ingenious experiments and built remarkable experimental devices to verify the results of their models. Yet when it comes to creating the "coherent understanding of the universe in its totality" that Teilhard felt the scientific profession must aspire, science's theoretical arm has reached an impasse—the barrier created by its adherence to a strictly external point of view.

We have discussed this obstacle to scientific progress before. A brief example will establish the idea in the present context. We begin with a look at the proton, which as we know is a constituent of the atomic nucleus and in the Standard Model of subatomic structure is composed of smaller particles called quarks. In order for the proton to hold together, its constituent quarks need to maintain a specific relationship to one another. Physicists recognize the importance of this relationship and postulate that a stream of intermediary particles called "gluons" travels between the quarks and conveys the "information" they need to maintain the correct alignment. Here the model begins to break down. How do the gluons interact with the quarks to convey information, and how do the quarks process and act on this information once they get it?

At the primitive evolutionary level represented by the proton, the line between matter and consciousness is blurred. Matter behaves less like "matter" than on later, more complex evolutionary levels. To pierce the external haze we need only envision the subatomic particle as the manifestation of an entity of consciousness in the act of perceiving another entity as the object of its need and by doing so establishing a relationship—the massless gluon particle and the spin, color, and charge characteristics of the quark our way of externally characterizing that interaction. Such a perspective, however, represents an internal model of subatomic structure, and science continues to resist such edifices. Instead, it favors probing the universe with increasingly complex and costly mathematical and experimental weapons. With each new assault, the barrier between internal and external strengthens, and the understanding that lies just beyond that barrier seems all the more elusive.

Our foray into the internal brings us to the area of human intellectual achievement where at present science prefers such a view remain, religion. Anthropologists define religion in a general way, as a shared system of beliefs. As such, a religion can be about most anything. Some have labeled today's rigid interpretation of science a religion. Others have labeled socialism, capitalism, and radical environmental and animal rights activism a religion. As we typically think of it, a religion is a shared system of beliefs that fulfills our need to understand our universe and ourselves by attributing the existence and behavior of such to a divine force or being.

So characterized, the world's major religions are based on what underneath the trappings of myth and ritual is a remarkably similar conception of "God." To most of us, God is understood to be some form of superior being. We see God as an entity whose consciousness is greater than our own. We see God as the creator, as an all-knowing and all-powerful being. As such, we also see God as an unchanging being.

The concept of an all-knowing, all-powerful, never-changing god creates certain dilemmas, above all the notion of "*good and evil*." If God is an all-knowing, all-powerful, never-changing entity, why would God unleash on humanity the suffering and ignorance that it has for so long endured? Would not an all-knowing, all-powerful, never-changing god see to it that we lived in a perfect world created by its perfect hand? Why does God not simply tell us the answers to life's questions?

To account for evil in the world, a religion must adopt certain supplementary notions. Foremost is the idea of "freewill." In one way or another, every major religion embraces the notion that the human being has the autonomy to conduct his or her affairs with or without God's approval. We can choose to align our lives with or against God's will. Though in most cases, God's will is somewhat hard to ascertain, and our lives are judged by the norms of religious propriety.

Also important among supporting concepts is the idea of an "evil force." To some degree, every religion attributes human suffering to the action of a force or being whose will opposes that of God—Satan, Lilith, Asmodeus, or other personification of evil or foe of good—demons versus angels. A person responsible for committing evil is said to be aligned with the entities of evil. The victim of evil is said to have drifted from his faith in God.

The problem with the concepts of freewill and evil force is that they erode the power of an all-knowing, all-powerful, never-changing God and thus the basis of religious philosophy. The notion of an all-knowing, all-powerful, never-changing God embodies the contradictions that negate its existence. Interestingly, when we set aside such a concept of the divine and look at "God" from the standpoint of an evolution of consciousness, the inconsistencies in its nature vanish.

In our view, we all consciously or unconsciously experience "God," for God is the consciousness that this book is devoted to understanding—the creative entity that we have come to know as the universe. As such, God is not an all-knowing, all-powerful, never-changing being but, as we have described, evolving to greater awareness through the cycles and thresholds and the trial and error of the creative process. God grows through the tribulations of the human experience. God is not a perfect being, but a being in the act of perfecting itself—or, as Teilhard characterized it, in the process of "Christogenesis."[1] Reflection invoked within God and humankind the ability to know one another. Since the moment they first pondered the other's existence, each has struggled to grasp their relationship. God is the consciousness that brought forth and embodies our existence and that is embodied within each of us.

Whether one accepts this or another view of God is a personal matter. What is clear is that, like evolution and natural selection, God and religion are not the same thing. God is what we experience, our sensation of interacting with a consciousness that in some way embraces our own. Religion is what we think about what we experience—the framework of concepts and the morality and mythology that we associate with God—with Buda, Jesus, Moses, Brahman, Mohamed, or other. As such, religion's highest aim, the nurturing of a relationship between God and the human being, is at times removed from religious practice. As profoundly uplifting and grounded in history and culture as certain aspects of religious practice may be, inconsistencies in philosophy compel the religious practitioner to devote creative energy to promoting ideology rather than to furthering

---

1. Teilhard used the term *Christogenesis* in a less than definitive way, to mean that God is in the act of evolution and to mean that humankind is in the act of evolving closer to God.

the unity between humanity and the universe the founders of that ideology may have envisioned it to achieve.

We evolve to greater consciousness and understanding by building on and creatively discarding old ideas to create new ideas. In the process of our growth, we turn to science and religion for answers, and they have the capacity to benefit our lives in this way. Yet, in many respects, science and religion are imprisoned in stagnation. Most scientists regard the human being as a product of natural selection, with no greater purpose than to reproduce. To many of these people, we are an out of balance species in the equilibrium works of a global biosystem—even a random mistake not to be repeated by nature. Similarly, religious explanations of the universe, most centuries from their inspiration, seem problematic and distant from the world we know. Rather than embrace ideology and doctrine as a path to God, many embrace ideology and doctrine over God. Like the universe of which science and religion are a part, the two towers of human intellect have drawn in on themselves, lost in the darkening cloud of our uncertainty.

Science and religion play an important role in our lives, but one that for the most part is secondary to the day-to-day concerns of existence. This brings us to the topic of economics. Because we devote the second book in the series, *Threshold to Meaning: Book 2, Economics of Fulfillment*, to the subject, we will leave the development and justification of the ideas that follow for that volume and limit our inquiry to the points and conclusions needed to further the present discussion.

We begin with certain basic concepts about economics. First, all contemporary systems of economic practice are scarcity-based. As the outgrowth of humankind's move to an urban way of life and the intrinsic state of scarcity it brought into being, all contemporary economic systems function on the assumption that resources are by nature limited and human material wants are by nature unlimited and that some mechanism must exist to encourage the production of goods and services and to regulate their allocation. Second, at the heart of any economic system—primitive, contemporary, and as we will see the economic systems of the future—is one factor—human creativity. Every economy exists as a result of our work, our energy, our dreams, our ambition, our skill, our drive, and our knowledge. What other than human creativity can underlie economic activity? Third, human creativity takes place within the individual. Corporations do not invent products. Individuals who work for corporations invent products. Government does not provide services. Individuals who work for government provide services. Machines may produce cars and circuit boards, but men and women design, build, and maintain the machines. Fourth, for the individual to contribute to the economy, one other variable must come into play—freedom. To express our creative vision and energy, we need room to work. We need resources and opportunity.

With the idea that today's global economy is scarcity-based and the idea that it is a human endeavor established, we turn to the two systems of allocation and production that dominate contemporary economic practice: *socialism* and *capitalism.*

In its theoretically pure form, socialism is based on the notion that we can best develop and allocate scarce resources by communal regulation of the means to produce and distribute wealth. In the socialist scheme, the individual creates goods and services in accordance with the governmentally determined needs of the community. The individual then turns over the wealth he or she produces to the community, which gives back what it feels the individual needs to subsist and continue to produce. Economic needs are accessed, economic activities are planned, and economic resources are allocated through central control.

One might think that in a planned economy it would be easy to meet everyone's needs. The government or some regulatory body simply mandates what to produce and how it should be distributed. In practice, this has not been the case, for a simple reason. To be human is to be creative. We are driven to grow and learn: to build a better life for ourselves and for our families. In a socialist economy, we exist to occupy a niche in the economic machine of the state. Our motivation is social conformity. By virtue of its central control, a socialist system stifles the freedom necessary for the individual to output the creative expression on which economic activity is fundamentally based. We all know or have been that bureaucrat who takes his break at the same time every day and does nothing more than what is in his job description.

Because socialism restricts the creative initiative of the individual, it is by nature a limited economic model. What socialist nation exists without a black market? The collective farms of the former Soviet Union were vast, but a disproportionate share of the nation's food was produced on tiny plots workers cultivated for themselves. In the 1980s, China's leaders realized that socialism could not survive in an ideologically pure form and opened their economy to business and investment. As the collapse of the Soviet Union and the stagnation of Cuba, North Korea, and other predominantly socialist nations make clear, in a socialistic economy, economic activity will invariably wind down and, as China's rulers hope to prevent, in the end collapse.

Today, most of us encounter socialism in the form of entitlements and other government social services. In this sense, every country employs a blend of socialistic and free-market economic practices. Some nations, as France and New Zealand, lean toward a planned economy. Others, as Taiwan and the United States, lean toward a market-driven economy. To whatever extent we may implement it, socialism cannot exist without a degree of capitalism.

This brings us to the economic model that most of us live and work within and that proponents claim offers the individual the freedom to exercise his or her creative power to the fullest extent of his or her abilities. When we look at capitalism in evolutionary context, the freedom it offers may be less tangible than we were indoctrinated to believe.

The capitalist model is based on the idea that we can best achieve our economic ends by letting our needs directly dictate economic activity—by the market. Whereas in socialism the individual has no motivation other than social conformity to contribute to the economy, in capitalism the individual has an economically direct motivation to contribute—*profit*, the ability to get more out of an economic activity than we put into it. Driven to turn a profit, we create or identify markets and supply goods and services targeted to those markets.

Central to this process is *capital*. Textbooks define capital as the body of goods and moneys from which we derive wealth, or a bigger body of goods and moneys. But capital means something more—*opportunity*. In a capitalist economy, control over capital gives the individual the means and freedom to raise a family, start a business, earn an education, market an invention, or in some way transform skills, dreams, and ambitions—as diverse as we may experience them—into activity and by doing so to earn a living and contribute to the economy.

The problem, of course, is that not everyone has access to capital and thus to the freedom and opportunity to contribute to the economy to the extent of his or her abilities. This is particularly true in a global economic environment. At one time, economic activities took place largely within a nation's territorial and thus legal boundaries, and government could to some extent oversee the availability of investment capital through fiscal and monetary policy and the regulation of banks and exchanges. More important, there was land and other non-monetary forms of capital available—the frontier. Today, capital changes hands with little regard to political borders, and virtually every resource has a monetary value. As important, political interests limit the availability of capital to favored economic segments. A multinational business may have no problem raising the money to open a factory or build a chain of retail stores. If a family who wants to start a small business can get a loan at all, they may have to secure it with their home.

The bottom line: capitalism cannot function without a mechanism to provide the average individual with access to capital, and overcoming the legal, cultural, and political barriers to creating a workable mechanism and the regulatory structure to support such a mechanism on the global scale of today's economy may not be possible, even desirable. By virtue of the profit motive and a greater acceptance of individuality, capitalism is a more vital way to conduct our economic affairs than socialism. None-the-less, it is a limited economic philosophy.

In every respect, the uncertainty of transition grips today's economy. Faced with tenuous global economic conditions and problems with capitalism and free markets, we seek solutions in socialism and governmental control. Faced with declining individual freedom and problems with socialism and governmental control, we seek solutions in capitalism and free markets. While the pendulum swings within the box of contemporary economic thought, living standards decline, economic injustice spreads, and governments increasingly challenge individual rights and ambitions. More and more human resources are devoted to tracking the flow of money and to playing the speculative games that fuel the markets and entangle the banking systems than to producing tangible goods and services. With each economic downturn—with each bubble the bursts, with each recession and or depression that is minimized or postponed—the economy behaves in ways pundits and economists cannot fathom and even less well informed politicians are powerless to control. In the play between free markets and central control, scarcity-based economics has brought humanity to where it stands but is obsolete, out-of-synch with our nature as evolving beings in an evolving universe—inapplicable to the souls we are becoming. Economics in all its past and contemporary forms is a product of an antiquated Darwinian, mechanistic view of the world:

a dogma, an ideology, a religion, a manifestation of the universe's age of understanding—a waning expression of an evolutionary era that draws to its end. Whereas economic philosophy should serve humanity, humanity slaves to the false profit of economic philosophy.

The obsolescence of modern economic practices has ramifications beyond our immediate material concerns. In part, these are apparent in what I call the Earth's *urban and ecological infrastructure*. This term encompasses the planet's natural and artificial ecosystems, the urban, industrial, and transportation network that overlays these ecosystems, and the human society woven into this network. As with the topic of economics, I will only highlight a few points and conclusions. We develop and justify our assertions in the third book in this series, *Threshold to Meaning: Book 3, Blueprint for Reconstruction*.

To paint with a broad stroke, today's urban and ecological infrastructure is shaped by two ideologically opposed forces. On one hand, we have economic interests, factions bent on extracting from the Earth the resources we need to go about our lives, with all the benefits and all the greed and exploitation this objective implies. Opposing this thrust of the human experience are environmental interests, factions bent on conservation and on limiting human activity and humankind's impact on the Earth. Just as contemporary economic doctrine is based on an obsolete, materialistic view of the world, so is contemporary environmental doctrine.

Many of us have a warm place in our heart for the environmental movement, and even the staunchest critic must concede that environmental activism has benefited our lives. In most developed nations, the air and water are cleaner today than they were half-a-century ago. Today's environmentalist, however, is not the environmentalist of the past. There are few if any John Muirs, Rachael Carsons, and Teddy and Franklyn Roosevelts. For reasons that as we mentioned we will justify in the later book, today's environmentalist embraces environmentalism in a different way, in a less altruistic manner—as an ideology.

Central to the environmental system of beliefs is a conception of nature derived from the idea of the ecosystem as it was popularly defined in the 1960s, a perspective where systems are seen as intricately functioning mechanisms that in their ideal state are in balance. As such, the biosphere is interpreted to be a vast machine where, prior to the ascent of civilization, every species interacted harmoniously with every other species—a complex, in-sync contrivance in an idyllic state of equilibrium.

The biosphere, however, has never been in a sustained state of equilibrium. It has been in a state of evolution. Moreover—since reflection, and potentially as far back as the great extinctions at the end of the Paleozoic—the net direction of the biosphere's evolution has been toward decline, toward a decrease in complexity and a reduction in the number of species and ecosystems. Unwilling to incorporate paleontology into their worldview, the environmental movement takes humanity to be that which has destroyed an idealized conception of nature. As such, we are the enemy. We are that which to save the deity of the Earth we must confront and in the end defeat.

Consequently, the dogma of environmental doctrine, which seeks to rollback the ecological clock, and the dogma of economic doctrine, which seeks to exploit the Earth, are at odds. The result is visible throughout the Earth's urban and ecological infrastructure. In the countryside, state and federal forestlands in the United States face fire, brush, and disease, and foresters blocked by legal bickering between business and environmental interests are powerless to improve forest health. In the city, private development and individual needs and tastes conflict with land use planning laws to create a dysfunctional automobile-based urban model. Commuters travel great distances between industrial and residential zones, and planners face the insurmountable challenge to design mass transit systems able to accommodate a city's politically distributed population. In the country and in the city, reason, science, and commonsense are powerless in a battle we wage between economic and environmental dogmas.

Caught in the struggle between obsolete worldviews is the human being. Throughout the industrial world, the individual often feels a lack of community. Neighbors do not know neighbors, and economic factors compel family members to live great distances apart. We are alone, isolated, ill suited to cope with the entrapment experienced when one is taken to be a commodity in a labor market or an evil that by virtue of the need to earn a living must be oppressed for the good of the Earth. With regard to economics, so ingrained is our belief in the human being as a component of the production process that in the United States pundits applaud the productivity of the American worker whose work week has soared and in the manufacturing and most other sectors of the economy whose inflation adjusted wages and job opportunities have for decades declined. With regard to environmentalism, so unquestioning are we of our belief in the malevolence of the human species that politicians are willing to sacrifice living standards in the developed world and condemn the third world to poverty in the name of global climate change while they dismiss technological solutions that can benefit humanity and the environment.

The uncertainty that grips the human experience manifests through obsolete economic and environmental doctrines, through urban design ill suited for human habitation, through personal alienation and lack of opportunity, and through families torn apart by economic stress and the values of central control and political conformity. Such is the decline of the Earth's urban and ecological infrastructure.

Today, we witness human suffering around the world and ask how much lack of vision can the human spirit endure. We face religious fundamentalism. We face scientific fundamentalism. We experience the human potential left to rot by economic and environmental doctrines that serve the few at the expense of practical solutions that benefit the many. To what depth must the storm of uncertainty that envelops the Earth batter our lives?

Uncertainty will collapse when the cycles of the creative process reach the point where the end of the universe's present evolutionary direction is no longer in doubt. As such, the answer to our question becomes apparent. The shroud of uncertainty that envelops the Earth need grow no darker than we permit. Humanity need sink into the belly of the whale no deeper than it allows.

When we come to this realization everything in life changes. Locked within our uncertainty is the motivation to lift humankind from its darkness. Held at bay by our fear of change is the energy to propel humanity to its immediate and ultimate future—beyond the age of understanding and into the universe's final evolutionary era, the period I call *Fulfillment*.

When we look back at the course of evolution, we see the remarkable effect created by the acceleration of time. Cosmic formation lasted perhaps 11 billion years. Yet, it took less than 4 billion years for the universe to advance through the age of life. And in these four billion years, mammals emerged only about 225 million years ago, and the earliest member of the human line emerged only about 7 million years ago. Humanity set out to comprehend itself and its world a mere 100 thousand years ago. We constructed the first settlements about 12 thousand years ago and invented modern science 300 years ago. The forces of evolution have drawn in on themselves to focus on a single point in time—the moment of the present. Reflection imparted the human need to create meaning. Today, the universe has reached the moment in its evolution where, through humanity's ascendance, it has the awareness to fulfill this need.

When we set aside our notions of a physical universe, we see creation in a way that is closer to its true nature. We come to know the universe as an entity of consciousness driven to advance to its ultimate form of existence. We recall its beginning in a state of emptiness. We look with wonder on its evolution. As we do, we find ourselves transformed. No longer are we merely a being that is self-aware. No longer are we merely a creature that is conscious of its own consciousness, endowed with the ability to ponder and contemplate. Our level of reflective consciousness becomes enwrapped within a higher level of awareness—a sentience of all time past, an internalization of evolution. Our awareness reaches out to embrace all that is the universe and all that is the universe's evolution. We grasp the nature of existence as it was, as it has become, and as it will become. We realize and accept our position as at the forefront of the universe's advance. We understand who we are and the purpose for our existence. Through our self-realization, the universe comprehends itself. The universe, through humanity, crosses the threshold to *Meaning*.

PART FIVE

Fulfillment

14

Perfection of Life on Earth

Tᴏᴅᴀʏ, ᴀꜱ I ᴡʀɪᴛᴇ these words, it is my belief that the universe is undergoing a fundamental evolutionary transformation—that humankind is crossing the threshold to the level of awareness I call meaning. To some the idea of meaning may seem fantasy. But to what end other than meaning can the universe's age of understanding lead? To what state other than wisdom must humanity's accumulation of knowledge achieve? As it did when we crossed the threshold to reflection, meaning will unfold within the individual and spread to bring forth a new order of humankind. We will look the same and in many ways behave the same, but the top level of human consciousness will be different. No longer will we be merely aware of our own awareness. In a manner no less fundamental, in a way no less ingrained than our capacity to reflect, we will be sentient of the universe as an evolution of consciousness. We will internalize the universe's origin, take as our own the universe's becoming. And, when we grasp within ourselves where we have been, we grasp within ourselves where we are headed. Guided by the wisdom of transcendence, humanity and the universe will share a common intent. Together, humanity and the universe will possess the drive and clarity to create their immediate and ultimate future. Endowed with the power of meaning, humanity and the universe will look back at their origin in emptiness. And, as they do, they will see and accept their need to create *fulfillment*.

As for humanity's immediate future in the universe's age of fulfillment, when the threshold to meaning unfolds, the social, economic, and military uncertainty we felt during the climax of the universe's age of understanding will vanish to become nothing more than a historical memory stored in our libraries and in what remain of the vast databanks that once dominated the human landscape. Motivated by our need to create fulfillment, we will take upon ourselves a profound goal. For no reason other than such is what the trial and error of fifteen billion years of evolution has nurtured us to achieve, we will commit ourselves to create fulfillment through the grandest of all undertakings—through the perfection of life on Earth.

Among the many aspects of life to be reshaped by our hand will be those embodied in the two great intellectual institutions we have traced since their origins: science and religion.

What will science be like twenty, thirty, or forty years from now? Although science has never been known to warmly embrace new ideas, we can say that, perhaps sooner than we may realize, the force of evolution will overcome the force of stagnation and science will reinvent itself.

The transformation to unfold within science will, as we have pointed out, center on the acceptance of the internal point of view. As scientists work with and understand this philosophical perspective, they will realize that it does not threaten the ideals of science nor the tradition embodied in those ideals. The view allows science to achieve its highest expression.

Theoretical science will enter a new age. Chemists and physicists will expand their models of time, space, matter, and energy. Biologists, anthropologists, and paleontologists will move beyond a Darwinian interpretation of organic evolution. Theoretical science will create what Teilhard felt only science has the capacity to achieve—the coherent understanding of the universe in its entirety that we, in these pages, have aspired to further.

Along with theoretical science, applied science will enter a new age. Humankind's perfection of life on Earth must on some level unfold through a reshaping of the physical world. This will require engineering on a scale never before seen, and science will provide the technology to support this endeavor. In the years ahead, the applied arm of science will occupy a special place in our lives. Much of our advancement will rest on focused research.

It is up to us whether science's transformation begins today or in the years to come. Such depends on those scientists willing to push back the boundaries of their disciplines and further the development of a vision of the universe that, guided by the cycles and thresholds of evolution, science has, for the two millennia of its existence, prepared itself to embrace.

Science, of course, is not the only institution dominated by rigid thought. In the years ahead, religion will also undergo a fundamental transformation.

Here I think change will be less apparent on the surface. Much of the ritual and pageantry we associate with religion will remain, for, if one is open to the indulgence, such activities do elevate the soul. Likewise, scripture and ideology will continue to fulfill a religious function. Without philosophical tradition there is little to sustain a religion's identity. What will change is the way the religious practitioner approaches ritual and scripture.

Religious writings and ceremony will no longer play an all-consuming role in spiritual life. Rites will become celebrations of religion's often troubled but often glorious past. Scripture will cease to be the undisputed word of God. We will come to view ritual and scripture as tributes to our struggle to understand the divine, as symbols of religion's sometimes misguided but ultimately cherished contribution to the human endeavor.

In the course of this transformation, religion will abandon its notion of an all-knowing, all-powerful, never-changing god. The fall of this ideal will lead to the collapse of the concept of good and evil as interpreted in the traditional theological sense and of the many ideas and actions such a dilemma fosters and justifies. We will no longer view God as an incomprehensible being, poised to judge our lives. Rather, we will come to know God in a personal way—as a companion, as a friend who like ourselves may stumble, but who will forever be there to guide and comfort—and to accept our guidance and comfort—as together we travel evolution's road.

Elevated by an evolution of consciousness view of God, religion will enter its most peaceful and important era. What more noble a cause can religion aspire than to nurture our well-being as in unity with the universe we set forth to perfect life on Earth.

Unstoppable are the cycles and thresholds of the creative process. Confronted with the power of meaning, the dogma and elitism that today grip scientific and religious life will wither into oblivion. Academic barriers will crumble, and religious fundamentalism will retreat into the chronicles of history. Science will enable us to fully grasp the nature of the universe, and religion will enable us to nurture a personal relationship with the universe.

In the years ahead, we will also reshape the many other institutions that touch our lives. Above all, humankind will move beyond socialism and capitalism and invent a new form of economics. We will engineer an economic philosophy that embraces our role in evolution and that integrates our nature as creative beings with our physical embodiment.

In the economics of tomorrow, the supposition of scarcity will have no meaning. From an evolution of consciousness standpoint, it makes no sense that the creative process would bring humanity to the realization of a greater endeavor on Earth without bringing forth the material potential and the creative power to achieve that endeavor. The economics of tomorrow will rest on the supposition of abundance—the notion that sufficient resources exist, or by our ingenuity can be made to exist, to allow humanity to further the greater endeavor of evolution.

In doing so, the economics of tomorrow will embrace the value of the individual. Our purpose is not Darwinian; it is not to survive and reproduce. We do not live to occupy a niche in the machine of global economics. Whatever economic system or systems we devise, the human being will not serve them. They will serve us. The universe evolves as we evolve. By virtue of our birth, by virtue of our place in evolution, we each play a role in creation. The universe cannot achieve its highest evolutionary state until every human being achieves his or her highest evolutionary state. Every human being—every man, woman, and child—has worth. We each have a place in creation. In the future, economic systems will exist solely for our benefit.

As such, the economy of tomorrow will maximize that which has always driven economic activity—that which the economic models of the past and present suppress or through the flow of capital seek to control and manipulate—the human drive to build and produce. We are compelled to better ourselves, to create greater awareness and well-being in our lives, to construct a better future for ourselves and our families. Our nature as creative beings in a creative universe motivates us to reshape our world. Human creativity and the opportunity to express that creativity is the driving force that generates external wealth and internal satisfaction.

In honor of the age before us, we will call our new economic philosophy *Economics of Fulfillment* and devote the second book in this series to its development. It is an ideology based on the notion that humanity can evolve to its potential only when every human being has the freedom and opportunity to evolve to his or her potential and that it is the human role and obligation to create the social and economic environment that allows this evolution to take place. We have the means and the responsibility to further our evolution.

Though of staggering impact, the economics of fulfillment philosophy is in many ways nothing more than the tool that will allow us to engage in an even more provocative endeavor. By ending the conflict and self-interest inherent in the scarcity-based economic practices of today, we create the freedom to engage in larger ventures. This includes the greatest of all engineering undertakings—the rebuilding of the Earth's urban and ecological infrastructure.

The objective of urban and ecological reconstruction will be to create a landscape that allows the individual to exercise his or her creative power and that—through the process of planning and construction—serves as an avenue for the individual's creative expression. To implement this goal, humanity must, as we have described, embrace a new economic philosophy, economics of fulfillment. Humanity must also embrace a new relationship with the environment. In the future, our goal will not be to exploit the Earth. Nor will it be to return the Earth to the imagined ideal of some past evolutionary state. The devolution of the Earth's biosphere began long ago. Humanity will take as its right and obligation the goal to manage this devolution in a way that meets our needs as evolving beings in an evolving universe. In the years ahead, we will move beyond notions of man and nature, Earth and environment and take command of evolution's trailing arrow.

Like today's rural and urban environments, tomorrow's rural and urban environments will reflect the human state of mind. In the countryside, we will have forests and wilderness areas, farms and rural communities. In the city, we will move beyond today's automobile-based urban model and embrace a design where the human energy that defines city life flows unimpeded within an urban matrix engineered to allow for its highest expression. The city and countryside of tomorrow will provide the individual with the freedom to choose the way of life he or she finds fulfilling. We will establish an environment that integrates diverse human activity into a coherent, aesthetic, and functional rural and urban framework.

Whatever form the trial and error of human creativity brings to the Earth's urban and ecological infrastructure, it will reflect and support our changing social needs. Free to grow and evolve as human beings, our social structure will continue its ascent out of collectivity. The family will gain new vigor, and greater mobility and economic freedom will allow the extended family to play an increasing role in our lives. In the years ahead, the human being will experience a never before felt sense of belonging.

Not only will the individual feel a part of his or her family, but of his or her community, city, and nation and of the body of humankind.

Today, the Earth's urban and ecological infrastructure reflects uncertainty in our lives. Tomorrow, it will reflect a sense of energy made possible by purpose, a sense of freedom made possible by organization. We will envision the Earth we want to live on, draw up a blueprint to create that Earth, and work together to transform our dream into reality. Toward this most inspiring of endeavors, we take the first step, small though it may be, in the third book in this series: *Blueprint for Reconstruction.* As the threshold to meaning unfolds, the individual will set forth into the future with a mission, for we each will play a role in the greater endeavor of the human ascent to fulfillment. Life on Earth cannot be perfected until it is perfected for and through the action of every human being.

The years ahead will be a time when we are exposed to new ideas and dream of the possibilities. But soon our ideas will take tangible form. Science and religion will reinvent themselves. We will create the first economic groups based on the economics of fulfillment philosophy. Groups will grow and merge to create the social, economic, and organizational framework we need to begin reconstruction of the Earth's urban and ecological infrastructure. The years will pass. Occupied in reengineering the planet, memories of war, poverty, and pollution will dim. The decades will pass. New cities will have arisen around the globe, and we will have forgotten life without meaning. The centuries will pass. Human existence will grow increasingly ideal. Then a time will come when humanity will have achieved what on crossing the threshold to meaning it had set out to do. Humankind will have accomplished its objective to perfect life on Earth. And, at the moment we do, uncertainty will build and collapse, and the universe will exhaust its potential to create fulfillment through the human endeavor on Earth. The universe will face yet another—even more startling—turning point in its evolutionary ascendance. Humankind will cross the threshold to its death.

15

Resurrection

IF THE THRESHOLD TO humankind's death that we spoke about at the end of the previous chapter was as it seemed, though, our existence would have no meaning. What point would there be for our notion of the creative process? What justification would we have for our view of an evolving God? Why dream of building great cities? Why dream of perfecting life on Earth? Why set forth into the future at all? If we were to see death as an end, would we not have regressed in our understanding of the universe? Would we not have returned to an age when we saw the cosmos as nothing more than matter, to a time when we saw the human being as nothing more than a machine? Whether one accepts the following discussion about life and afterlife is a personal issue. But the existence of human consciousness beyond life and the consequence such holds for the universe's future is a joyous outcome of the evolution of consciousness view.

To understand how human consciousness could continue beyond the sphere of existence we associate with the physical universe, we begin by returning to an early point in evolution. We travel back to an era when organic development was at a primitive stage.

As you may recall, lifespan—or genetically programmed death—emerged in the unicellular life form about 1.2 billion years ago. The advent of predetermined death came about as a result of time-acceleration, the quickening of the universe's evolution. Death became the mechanism through which the creative process more rapidly discarded life's obsolete designs. For eons, evolution locked in the complexification of organic form. Birth and death marked the flow of evolutionary progress. Then at that remarkable moment one hundred thousand years ago when the universe crossed the threshold to reflection and the ability to ponder and contemplate emerged within what we can now properly call humanity, death took on a new meaning.

The threshold to reflection created what we can think of as a symmetry break in the human psyche, a divide in evolution. The human body consists of systems of consciousness and creative activity nestled within systems of consciousness and creative activity. The threshold to reflection wrapped what was our previous top level of consciousness and creative function, that manifest as our ability to deal with the world abstractly, within a new level of consciousness and creative function, that manifest as our ability to deal with the world reflectively.

Reflective consciousness exists above organic structure. The human being maintains an internal representation of its world made-up of states of comprehension, states of the individual's consciousness as opposed to awareness associated with organic structure of perception. Our level of reflective consciousness interacts with our level of abstract consciousness and thus with all lower levels of body awareness, but it exists removed from these levels. We maintain and exist within a time-space framework of our own making. With reflection, the individual attained the autonomy to exist as a self-aware being—as an independent universe in the greater scheme of creation. We achieved the consciousness to embody, or more correctly, to exist as a soul.

The threshold to reflection imparted the recognition of death. It also imparted the ability to maintain the essential awareness that constitutes human existence beyond life. Death is a transition, a breaking away of the essential self from the physical self. Our passing from the realm of existence we associate with life takes place when our bodies no longer maintain the link between our level of reflective awareness and our level of abstract awareness. On death, the top level of human consciousness, the consciousness that is the soul, separates from the structure of perception that is the body. Afterlife is an aspect of the human ability to reflect, a dimension of who we are. Its existence and our ability to pass into the sphere of reality we associate with it are qualities of our humanity. To deny an afterlife is to deny the uniqueness of our being.

If our essential self continues after death, it is natural to ask what our existence down the road will be like. What will we feel, think, and experience in the afterlife? For obvious reasons, the particulars of our experience in the afterlife must await the time of our passing. But the view of the universe we have developed does allow us to make certain conjectures.

In life, our level of abstract consciousness lends structure to our level of reflective consciousness. We experience a world defined by physical time, space, and movement and maintain a reflective representation of that world based on our experience. As important, our world overlaps with the worlds experienced by those around us. As diverse as our personal and cultural experiences may be, they are shaped by and contribute to an overall human experience of existence. Through our ability to communicate and to perceive one another as the object of our need, we exist within and contribute to a framework of human consciousness.

On death, our link to the physical world ends but our link to the framework of human consciousness remains. This link, however, is no longer channeled through our experience of the physical world. The sphere of reality we associate with life is dominated by the fifteen-billion-year-old structure of the universe's pre-reflective evolution. The sphere of reality we associate with afterlife is dominated by the one-hundred-thousand-year-old structure of humanity's reflective evolution. In the afterlife, we can expect to find ourselves embodied in a physical form, or to experience ourselves as such, and to be able to move within a physical reality. Creative activity manifests in time and space. But, because the afterlife rests on a time-space fabric not directly associated with the universe's physical construct, it would be less rigid. Laws of matter and energy would apply less rigorously. Social and cultural structures would embrace more intimately. On death, we face neither mythical hell or heaven nor scientific oblivion but familiar human need and uncertainty in a landscape far more free and vivid.

When we take existence beyond life into account, we see the universe as an entity of consciousness comprised of two regions: life and afterlife. Life embraces the human experience in a construct of physical evolution. Afterlife embraces the human experience in a construct of human consciousness, a reflective matrix of existence. Our recognition of this dichotomy within the universe profoundly advances our view of evolution.

From the standpoint of the individual, the death of others compels us to ponder the nature of our existence. When faced with the death of one who is close, we stop what we are doing and ask what significance that person's life may have held—what purpose that person's death may have served. Death forces us to ask the fundamental human questions. It draws us out of our shell of triviality to, if only for a moment, drive us to contemplate a greater meaning. The death of others spurs our sometimes lethargic urge to further our personal evolution.

Likewise, our own death marks a profound moment in our evolution. Death forces us to reevaluate our deepest notions of who we are and for what purpose we came into existence—concepts etched into our being by a lifetime faced with the realities of a physical universe. Even though our transition into afterlife may temporarily separate us from loved ones and that separation may be painful, death is a time of renewal, a moment when we as human beings are free to reinvent ourselves—when we are free to creatively discard the old.

From the standpoint of the universe, life is the sphere of reality where new human beings are born into existence. In life, the ancient process of organic reproduction brings forth new souls to take their place in creation. Afterlife is the sphere of reality where human consciousness rises above the bounds of the physical, where human awareness entwines to create an orb of reflective thought. We share the afterlife with beings born throughout the ages. We may even meet that person who first crossed the threshold to reflection. So much that person must have experienced during a hundred millennia of existence. So much that person must have to tell.

When we incorporate the existence of afterlife into our framework of evolution, we grasp the universe's true scope and grandeur. Afterlife came into being with reflection. Evolution brought into existence a universe characterized by the birth of human consciousness in life, by the flow of human consciousness across the barrier of death, and by the massing of human consciousness in afterlife. We see in the universe an architecture that evolved to bring forth awareness. We see in the universe a structure engineered to further evolution.

As scripture and archeology attest, humankind has for at least one hundred thousand years accepted the existence of a soul and afterlife. The diversity of our beliefs show that we held many views on their nature, but that in one form or another we took their existence to be self-evident. Only in the last 150 or so years have we questioned these most established of human notions. Only in the age of science and so-called reason have we dared to think of the human being as a machine that on death turns off. How, in the evolution of consciousness view, where awareness is that which is solid and matter is that which is transient and reflects the movement of awareness, can existence beyond life not be the true state of affairs? In our hearts, do we really feel death is the end? Do we really believe there is nothing more?

Today, the threshold to meaning unfolds within humankind. With it comes a sense of power and serenity. We no longer need fear nor sanctify death. We have evolved the capacity to accept death for what it is: a turning point in our development, a functional aspect of who we are and of the universe's evolution. Life is the first stage in our existence, the period of our gestation in a universe more grand and expansive than any we could have imagined.

Just as the individual must face death, humanity must face death. In the decades and centuries ahead, the barrier between life and death will weaken as we come to accept and understand that barrier. Then, however many centuries or millennia down the road it may be, humanity will reach the moment when it achieves what, on crossing the threshold to meaning, it had set out to do—perfect life on Earth. At that instant, the universe will reach the point where the catalytic function of life and afterlife will have exhausted its evolutionary usefulness. The boundary between life and death will fall into evolution's trailing arrow and vanish from existence. The sphere of reality that is life and the sphere of reality that is afterlife will unite, and the universe will achieve the consciousness to create its ultimate future.

16

The Omega Point

WITH DEATH BANISHED TO obsolescence and humanity unified in an existence unfettered by the limits of the physical universe, the uncertainty associated with another, still more profound evolutionary transformation will grip the human experience. Stagnation will increase, and the dark side of the creative force will mount its last onslaught. The creative process will mass the energy needed to propel the universe to its ultimate state of existence. Aligned with humankind, the universe will achieve the awareness to cross the threshold to its final evolutionary form.

In this book, we began our depiction of the universe's evolution with a simple if not self-evident supposition, the notion that the universe originated in a state of emptiness.

We derived a definition of emptiness, self-evident in its own right, and inferred from our definition that the universe began as a rudimentary consciousness, as a primordial awareness of the need for and of the uncertainty as to how to create fulfillment.

Based on our definition of emptiness and on our inference about the universe's origin, we developed a model to explain how the universe evolved as an entity of expanding consciousness. We called this model the creative process and described its function as taking place through cycles of perception and external manifestation, through the growth and collapse of uncertainty, and through the crossing of thresholds to higher evolutionary stages.

We expanded our model of the creative process to account for creative activity in two directions. The leading arrow of the creative process drives evolution forward. The trailing arrow reshapes and discards prior evolutionary forms in support of evolution's continued advance. The creative process builds on and creatively discards the old to create the new.

In our view of evolution, emptiness is the fundamental driving force behind the becoming that is the universe, the sole and essential energy that motivates creation. The creative process is the mechanism through which that energy translates into evolution. It is the system of interaction through which the consciousness that is the universe and the consciousness that is embodied within the universe advance to greater autonomy and awareness.

Along with our introduction to the creative process, we progressed stage-by-stage through the universe's evolution. We called the first of the universe's major evolutionary periods the age of *Emergence*. Here, from an internal point of view, we saw the universe's evolution unfold as an expansion of consciousness followed by the doubling of the entity of consciousness that resulted. From an external point of view, we saw the universe's evolution unfold as an expansion of space and uniform energy followed by the doubling of the region of space and uniform energy that resulted. Emergence climaxed as the universe crossed the threshold to the form that would allow it to further evolve—the threshold of *Autonomy in Unity*.

We called the universe's second major evolutionary period the age of *Structure*. From an internal point of view, we saw evolution progress as the autonomous entities of consciousness from which the universe was composed perceived one another as the object of their need and, by doing so, created relationships. Relationships, in turn, perceived one another as object to create successively more consciousness arrangements. The universe advanced as its structure of perception became more complex and the aspects of consciousness from which it was composed became more autonomous and aware. From an external point of view, we saw the universe's evolution progress as particles formed clusters of particles and as clusters of particles formed more complex structural units, giving rise to atoms, molecules, the cosmos, organic molecules, and simple metabolic systems. The universe's age of structure climaxed with the emergence of the first cell, the first entity capable of reproduction. The universe marked the line between life and pre-life. It crossed the threshold of *Design Over Structure*.

We called the universe's third major evolutionary period the age of *Life*. During this period, the universe evolved to greater awareness through the design of the Earth's biosphere and the life that it embodied. By way of the cycles and thresholds, the trial and error, and the creative building on and discarding of the old of the creative process, increasingly complex and conscious life-forms emerged, and the Earth advanced into and through the Paleozoic, the Mesozoic, and the Cenozoic. Ecosystems became more intricate and realigned in support of continued evolution. Sex and lifespan appeared. Sleep and dream developed, and abstract thought emerged and intensified. Social structure became less collective. Behavior grew more spontaneous. Personality grew more distinct, and physical form grew more versatile. About seven million years ago, evolution's leading edge locked in the advancement of the human line. About one hundred thousand years ago, human awareness rose above the level of organic structure, and the universe marked a profound turning point in its evolution—the threshold to *Reflection*.

We characterized the moment of humankind's first reflective thought as the instant when the universe stood face-to-face with itself. That first look at itself created an overpowering need to comprehend itself. Through the power of human creativity, the universe set out to grasp the nature and purpose of its existence—to create meaning. Our depiction of evolution entered the universe's fourth major evolutionary period, the age we called *Understanding*.

Moreover, our quest to create understanding took place in a universe that had taken on a new form. With the threshold to reflection, the human being achieved the autonomy to exist independent of the greater universe—as a universe in itself. This gave rise to a reality defined by two spheres of existence—life and afterlife—and by the flow of human consciousness between. Spurred by time-acceleration, the universe had reinvented itself. The universe had molded its structure into a form that given its reflective existence would further its evolution.

Threshold after threshold, human understanding grew. In the sphere of the living, we invented gods and religions, created art, myth, and ritual. We built cities, states, nations, and empires. We developed writing and mathematics, pondered the heavens, and probed the physical universe. A little over two thousand years ago, we saw the world in terms of the internal and external point of view, and our knowledge of the universe's physical dimension increased at an accelerated rate. We invented new materials and forms of warfare. We saw the Earth as revolving around the sun, sailed the world's oceans, and mapped its continents. We founded the scientific method, recognized the existence of evolution, and formulated the laws of classical mechanics. The universe evolved to greater awareness as humankind evolved to a greater understanding of its place in creation.

The discoveries made in the twentieth century and the turmoil that took place during that period thrust humanity to a state of global consciousness, to an internalization of the noosphere. They also brought us to the point where we stand today and to the central contention of our account of the universe and its becoming. Stage-by-stage, our analysis led us to a conclusion—to an unavoidable outcome of the evolution of consciousness view. As Teilhard foretold and as we described, the universe today crosses the most profound evolutionary threshold since the emergence of reflective consciousness more than a thousand lifetimes ago.

Human knowledge has accumulated without limit. Today, the understanding represented by that knowledge makes it possible for us to fulfill a long established evolutionary goal. Today, the universe embodies the consciousness to achieve what it had set out to do the moment the first human being pondered his or her existence. We recognize the internal nature of the universe. We understand that the universe began in a state of emptiness and that the universe's motivation is to create the consciousness that will allow it to resolve this sense of void. We embrace the universe's becoming. Today, the universe crosses the threshold to *Meaning*.

Empowered by this awareness, we set forth into the universe's final evolutionary era, the age we called *Fulfillment*. Today, we step into an era where wisdom and creative growth define the human experience, and our awareness of who we are and of where we are headed aligns our creative energy to the task of perfecting life on Earth. We will redefine the limits of science and reinterpret the nature of God and religion. We will invent a new economics, take command of evolution's trailing arrow, and rebuild the Earth's urban and ecological infrastructure in support of the universe's continued evolution.

Today, we also step into an era that has an ultimate outcome. In the distant future, when the boundary between the living and those who have passed has fallen into obsolescence, and the sphere of life and the sphere of afterlife have become one, uncertainty will build for the last time. One final moment of doubt will grip creation. Evolution's leading arrow exists only in the present. To become what it must, the universe must abandon all that it has been. With the acceptance of this insight, with the willingness to let go of all that has past, uncertainty will collapse. The energy held at bay by that uncertainty will propel the universe through its last evolutionary transformation—across the threshold to its final evolutionary form.

Life and Earth will fall from existence. From the memories of physical creation, a structure of ultimate non-collectivity will rise. We will each become as the universe, and the universe will become as each of us. We will each perceive the universe and all other human beings as the object of our need. We will each embrace and be embraced by the creative cycles of all others. As our creative process supports and is supported by the creative process of all other entities of existence, consciousness will have reached its potential. Uncertainty will no longer grow. The creative process will no longer bring forth evolution. Time will flow but not accelerate. Space will manifest satisfaction. We will exist as hyper-unique beings, entities on a level of consciousness equal to all others and to the universe. Ultimate autonomy will sustain ultimate unity. Just as no state less evolved than the universe's original state of emptiness can exist, no state more evolved than the universe's final state of self-convergence can be achieved. The universe will have perfected itself. It will have reached the level of awareness Teilhard called the "Omega Point." No longer will the universe be alone. Together, humanity and the universe will have created the consciousness necessary to sustain their fulfillment.

17

Two Worlds

THE 1955 PUBLICATION OF Teilhard's *The Phenomenon of Man* brought to light the evolution of consciousness view. Inspired by this view, it is my belief that today the universe is crossing an evolutionary threshold and that this threshold represents the most deeply felt transformation since the emergence of reflective consciousness more than one hundred thousand years ago. Like the universe's turning point to reflection, the evolutionary rebirth now underway unfolds within humankind. The state of wisdom we call meaning has blossomed within us. We live during the rarest of times, the moment of transformation between two worlds.

In the future lies the universe's age of fulfillment—warm, provocative, poised to embrace the Earth, compelling us to look toward our upcoming and ultimate stages of existence. When we look ahead, we see the emergence of a new economic philosophy—a way of life based on the principle that humanity, and thus the universe, can achieve its potential only when every human being has the freedom and opportunity to achieve his or her potential. When we look ahead, we see perfection of life on Earth—the rebuilding of the Earth's urban and ecological infrastructure and the emergence of a less collective and more intimate family, community, and global social organization. Fulfillment is a transitory experience, sustained by the power of need through the cycles and thresholds of the creative process. It requires creation, and we require an environment where we can engage in that creation. The world of the future promises to be such a place.

Yet, the universe's current era, the age of understanding, tightens its grip on the planet—familiar, accepted, compelling us to look toward the world we know. In the present, we find socialism and capitalism—economic ideologies based on the idea of scarce resources. We find urban and ecological decay, information valued over wisdom, and the accumulation of wealth valued over creativity and the production of wealth. We find the breakdown of family and community and the growth of a world order dominated by central control and economic class. The creative process builds on and discards the old to create the new. Inherent within this process is our reluctance to abandon long-standing ideas and established ways of doing things. The world of today offers a way of life gripped by stagnation, but one in which we are familiar.

Caught in the uncertainty of our time, we yearn for meaning in our lives. With our recognition of this need, and with our first step toward its realization, we begin a transformation of the soul. Our life aligns with the flow of the universe and with the lives of others on the same path. Insight by insight, our understanding of the universe and of ourselves grows. Ultimately, we reach a point where we realize that meaning is more than the ideas and concepts that guided us in our quest, more than the knowledge and understanding that we acquired on our journey. Meaning is a personal state of existence, a level of consciousness unique to every individual. With this realization, meaning unfolds and it is our own.

Today, the universe exists at the moment of transformation between two evolutionary eras. With meaning, we recognize our need for fulfillment and direct our creative energy toward its resolution. The gate to a new world opens. We step forward. We pause and reflect. Within each of us lies the universe's origin. Within each of us lies the universe's evolution. Within each of us lies the universe's threshold to reflection and threshold to meaning. On birth, we became part of the great movement that is the universe. We set forth on a journey that has carried us through life and that will carry us into afterlife. Through each of us, the universe advances. And when we each in our own way arrive, we and the universe will achieve the consciousness to create our ultimate future.

Bibliography

Ashby, W. Ross. *An Introduction to Cybernetics*. New York: Methuen and Company, 1964.

Ashby, W. Ross. *Design for a Brain*. New York: John Wiley and sons, 1952.

Barnett, Lincoln. *The Universe and Dr. Einstein*. New York: Time Incorporated, 1962.

Bergson, Henri. *Creative Evolution*. Translated by Arthur Mitchell. New York: The Modern Library, 1944.

Bergson, Henri. *The Creative Mind*. Translated by Mabelle L. Andison. New York: Greenwood Press, 1968.

Bergson, Henri. *Time and Free Will: An Essay on the Immediate Data of Consciousness*. Translated by F. L. Pogson. New York: Greenwood Press, 1968.

Bertalanffy, Ludwick Von. *General System Theory: Foundations, Development, Applications*. New York: George Braziller, 1968.

Bloom, Howard. *Global Brain: The Evolution of Mass Mind from the Big Bang to the 21st Century*. New York: John Wiley & Sons, 2001.

Bloom, Howard. *The Lucifer Principle: A Scientific Investigation into the Forces of History*. New York: Atlantic Monthly Press, 1997.

Bramblett, Claud A. *Patterns of Primate Behavior*. Palo Alto, CA: Mayfield Publishing Company, 1976.

Brown, Theodore L., et. al. *Chemistry: The Central Science, 6th ed*. Englewood Cliffs, NJ: Prentice Hall, 1994.

Calvin, William. *The ascent of Mind: Ice Age Climates and the Evolution of intelligence*. New York: Bantam, 1990.

Campbell, Bernard G. *Humankind Emerging, 7th ed*. New York: HarperCollins, 1996.

Campbell, Joseph. *The Hero with a Thousand Faces*. Princeton, NJ: Princeton University Press, 1968.

Capra, Fritjof. *The Hidden Connections: A Science for Sustainable Living*. New York: Anchor, 2004.

Capra, Fritjof. *The Tao of Physics: An Exploration of the Parallels between Modern Physics and Eastern Mysticism*. New York: Bantam, 1975.

Capra, Fritjof. *The Turning Point: Science, Society, and the Rising Culture*. New York: Bantam, 1984.

Capra, Fritjof. *The Web of Life: A New Scientific Understanding of Living Systems*. New York: Anchor, 1997.

Conant, Roger. *Mechanics of Intelligence: Ross Ashby's Writings on Cybernetics*. Seaside, CA: Intersystems Publications, 1981.

Dawkins, Richard. *The God Delusion*. New York: Mariner Books, 2008.

Delfgaauw, Bernard. *Evolution: The Theory of Teilhard de Chardin*. Translated by Hubert Hoskins. New York: Harper and Row, 1969.

Bibliography

Dodson, Edward O. *The Teilhardian Synthesis, Lamarckism & Orthogenesis*. Lewisburg, VA: American Teilhard Association, 1993.

Dodson, Edward O., et al. *Creation or Evolution: Correspondence on the Current Controversy*. Ottawa: University of Ottawa Press, 1990.

Dubos, René. *Celebrations of Life*. New York: McGraw-Hill, 1981.

Farb, Peter. *Humankind: What We Know About Ourselves. Where We Came From And Where We Are Headed. Why We Behave The Way we do*. New York: Bantam, 1978.

Foote, Michael and Arnold I. Miller. *Principles of Paleontology*. New York: W. H. Freeman, 2006.

Franklin, Jon. *Writing for Story: Craft Secrets of Dramatic Nonfiction by a two-time Pulitzer Prize Winner*. New York: Dutton, 1994.

Futuyma, Douglas J. *Evolution*. Sunderland, MA: Sinauer Associates, 2005.

Gardner, John. *The Art of Fiction*. New York: Vintage, 1985.

Giere, Ronald N. *Understanding scientific reasoning, 3rd ed.* Austin, TX: Holt, Rinehard, and Winston, 1991.

Grenet, Paul. Teilhard de Chardin: *The Man and His Theories*. Translated by R. A. Rudorff. London: Souvenir Press, 1965.

Hawking, Steven. *A Brief History of Time*. New York: Bantam, 1998.

Hook, Sidney. *Dimensions of Mind*. New York: Collier Books, 1961.

Hurley, Patrick J. *A Concise Introduction to Logic, 5th ed.* Belmont, VA: Wadsworth Publishing Company, 1994.

Huxley, Julian. *New Bottles for New Wine*. New York: Harper and Brothers, 1957.

Jantsch, Erich. *Design for Evolution: Self-Organization and Planning in the Life of Human Systems*. New York: Braziller, 1975.

Jantsch, Erich. *The Evolutionary Vision: Toward a Unifying Paradigm of Physical, Biological, and Sociocultural Evolution*. Boulder, CO: Westview Press for the American Association for the Advancement of Science, 1981.

Jantsch, Erich. *The Self-Organizing Universe: Scientific and Human Implications of the Emerging Paradigm of Evolution*. New York: Pergamon Press, 1980.

Jones, Steven, et. al. *The Cambridge Encyclopedia of Human Evolution*. Cambridge, UK: Cambridge University Press, 1992.

King, Ursula. *Christ in All Things: Exploring Spirituality with Teilhard de Chardin*. Maryknoll, NY: Orbis Books, 1997.

King, Ursula. *Christian Mystics: Their Lives and Legacies throughout the Ages*. Mahwah, NJ: Paulist Press, 2001.

King, Ursula. *Pierre Teilhard de Chardin: Writings*. Maryknoll, NY: Orbis Books, 1999.

King, Ursula. *Spirit of Fire: The Life and Vision of Pierre Teilhard de Chardin*. Maryknoll, NY: Orbis Books 1998.

King, Ursula. *Spirituality and Society in the New Millennium*. Sussex, UK: Sussex Academic Press, 2001.

King, Ursula. *Turning Points in Religious Studies*. London: Continuum International Publishing Group, 2000.

Krane, Kenneth. *Modern Physics, 2nd ed.* New York: John Wiley & Sons, 1996.

Lane, David. *The Phenomenon of Teilhard: Prophet for a New Age*. Macon, GA: Mercer University Press, 1996.

Lyon, William and Wallace Black Elk. *Black Elk: The Sacred Ways of a Lakota*. San Francisco: HarperCollins, 1990.

Lyon, William. *Encyclopedia of Native American Heeling*. Oxford, UK: ABC-CLIO, 1996.

Bibliography

Neihardt, John. *Black elk speaks*. New York: William Morrow and Company, 1932.

Norris, Robert E. and L. Lloyd Haring. *Political Geography*. New York: Charles E. Merril and Company, 1980.

Ortega y Gasset, José. *The Revolt of the Masses*. New York: W. W. Norton and Company, 1960.

Peterson, Willis. *Principles of Economics, 4th ed*. Homewood, IL: Richard D. Irwin, 1980.

Pletsch, Carl. *Young Nietzsche: Becoming a Genius*. New York: The Free Press, 1991.

Prigogine, Ilya and Isabelle Stengers. *Order Out of Chaos*. New York: Bantam, 1984.

Prothero, Donald R. *Bringing Fossils to Life: An Introduction to Paleobiology*. New York: McGraw Hill, 2003.

Resnick, Robert and David Halliday. *Basic Concepts in Relativity Theory and Early Quantum Mechanics*. Englewood Cliffs, NJ: Prentice Hall, 1991.

Russell, Bertrand. *The ABC of Relativity*. New York: Signet, 1925.

Serway, Raymond A. *Principles of Physics*. New York: Harcourt, 1994.

Stringer, Chris and Peter Andrews. *The Complete World of Human Evolution*. London: Thames and Hudson, 2005.

Teilhard de Chardin, Pierre. *Activation of Energy*. Translated by Rene Hague. London: Collins, 1970.

Teilhard de Chardin, Pierre. *Building the Earth*. Translated by Noel Lindsay. Wilkes-Barre, PA: Dimension Books, 1965.

Teilhard de Chardin, Pierre. *Christianity and Evolution*. Translated by Rene Hague. New York: Harcourt Brace Jovanovich, 1971.

Teilhard de Chardin, Pierre. *Early Man of China*. New York: AMS Press, 1980.

Teilhard de Chardin, Pierre. *Human Energy*. Translated by J. M. Cohen. London: Collins, 1969.

Teilhard de Chardin, Pierre. *Hymn of the Universe*. Translated by Gerald Vann. New York: Harper and Row, 1961.

Teilhard de Chardin, Pierre. *Let Me Explain*. Edited by Jean-Pierre Demoulin. Translated by Rene Hague. London: Collins, 1970.

Teilhard de Chardin, Pierre. *Letters From a Traveller*. New York: Harper and Row, 1962.

Teilhard de Chardin, Pierre. *Letters to Two Friends*. 1926–1952: New York: New American Library, 1968.

Teilhard de Chardin, Pierre. *Man's Place in Nature*. Translated by Rene Hague. New York: Harper and Row, 1966.

Teilhard de Chardin, Pierre. *On Love and Happiness*. San Francisco: Harper and Row, 1984.

Teilhard de Chardin, Pierre. *Science and Christ*. Translated By Rene Hague. New York: Harper and Row, 1968.

Teilhard de Chardin, Pierre. *The Appearance of Man*. Translated by Robert T. Francoeur. New York: Harper and Row, 1965.

Teilhard de Chardin, Pierre. *The Divine Milieu: An Essay on the Interior of Life*. New York: Harper and Row, 1960.

Teilhard de Chardin, Pierre. *The Future of Man*. Translated by Norman Denny. New York: Harper and Row, 1964.

Teilhard de Chardin, Pierre. *The Heart of the Matter*. Translated by Rene Hague. New York: Harcourt Brace Jovanovich, 1979.

Teilhard de Chardin, Pierre. *The Letters of Teilhard de Chardin and Lucile Swan*. Edited by Mary W. Gilbert. Washington, DC: Georgetown University Press, 1993.

Bibliography

Teilhard de Chardin, Pierre. *The Making of a Mind: Letters from a Soldier-Priest, 1914–1919*. Translated by Rene Hague. New York: Harper and Row, 1965.

Teilhard de Chardin, Pierre. *The Phenomenon of Man*. Translated by Bernard Wall. New York: Harper and Row, 1959.

Teilhard de Chardin, Pierre. *The Vision of the Past*. Translated by J. M. Cohen. London: Collins, 1966.

Teilhard de Chardin, Pierre. *Toward the Future*. Translated By Rene Hague. New York: Harcourt Brace Jovanovich, 1975.

Teilhard de Chardin, Pierre. *Writings in Time of War*. Translated By Rene Hague. New York: Harper and Row, 1968.

Wilson, David Sloan. *Evolution for Everyone: How Darwin's Theory Can Change the Way We Think About Our Lives*. New York: Delacorte, 2007.

Zimmer, Carl. *Smithsonian Intimate Guide to Human Origins*. New York: Harper Collins, 2005.